Understanding the Global Market

Navigating the International Business Environment

Bruce D. Keillor

 PRAEGER

AN IMPRINT OF ABC-CLIO, LLC
Santa Barbara, California • Denver, Colorado • Oxford, England

Copyright 2013 by ABC-CLIO, LLC

All rights reserved. No part of this publication may be reproduced, stored in a retrieval system, or transmitted, in any form or by any means, electronic, mechanical, photocopying, recording, or otherwise, except for the inclusion of brief quotations in a review, without prior permission in writing from the publisher.

Library of Congress Cataloging-in-Publication Data

Keillor, Bruce David.
 Understanding the global market : navigating the international business environment / Bruce D. Keillor.
  p. cm.
 Includes bibliographical references and index.
  ISBN 978-1-4408-0301-7 (hardcover : alk. paper) — ISBN 978-1-4408-0302-4 (ebook)
 1. International economic relations. 2. International trade. 3. International business enterprises. I. Title.
  HF1359.K417 2013
  658'.049—dc23   2012037235

ISBN: 978-1-4408-0301-7
EISBN: 978-1-4408-0302-4

17 16 15 14 13 1 2 3 4 5

This book is also available on the World Wide Web as an eBook.
Visit www.abc-clio.com for details.

Praeger
An Imprint of ABC-CLIO, LLC

ABC-CLIO, LLC
130 Cremona Drive, P.O. Box 1911
Santa Barbara, California 93116-1911

This book is printed on acid-free paper ∞

Manufactured in the United States of America

To Gretchen, Jonathan, and Jeremy,

three of the best writers I know

Contents

Preface

Unlike many other books dealing with international business, this is not a "how-to" approach for developing a successful strategy. Instead, this book specifically addresses what many others often treat in a less than comprehensive manner—that is, the various facets of the international business environment. The overall purpose of *Understanding the Global Market* is to provide a practitioner-oriented, easily understood guide to this complex, multilayered international business environment. It differs from other books currently on the market in two ways: first, this is a comprehensive approach to dealing with *all* aspects of the international business environment, not just the more recognizable, such as culture. Second, in this book, we focus on the unique characteristics *of* international markets and their effect on international operations, as opposed to a firm's attitude toward its operating position *in* international markets.

In the first chapter, I begin first not by exploring the international business environment but by coming to grips with the various objectives any given firm might seek to achieve in its international operations. The premise is simple: it is impossible to accurately assess any market's environment when the firm has no clear idea what it is trying to accomplish in that market. Along the way, we will also consider why being "international" may not be an option, as well as the unique challenges that firms face when operating outside of their domestic market. In subsequent chapters, we investigate the cultural environment and how best to connect with customers and employees, the physical environment and how to choose and enter a market, the economic environment and its impact on market attractiveness, the political environment and how the rules for doing business are created, and the competitive environment and how to succeed over time. We then move to how a firm might have an impact on the market in which it operates—and how to manage that impact—and some important aspects of the future international environment. The book concludes with a framework for systematically analyzing the international business environment.

Understanding the Global Market is for firms and managers of all types, ranging from those contemplating a move into the global market to those seeking to improve their international operations. By using a combination of established conceptual frameworks, practical perspectives of analysis and assessment, and real-world examples, this book provides a cutting-edge approach to dealing with the various complex challenges firms face when "going international." It is absolutely vital for any business involved in international markets to systematically analyze all pieces of its market environment, and this book provides the means for accomplishing this goal. Best of luck in all your international efforts, and enjoy *Understanding the Global Market*!

CHAPTER ONE

The International Business Environment: An Overview and New Perspectives (Complexities and Choices)

Introduction

Because of the ever-increasing interdependence of markets around the globe, there is a real need for businesses of all sizes—and in all countries—to consider the opportunities expanding into this global marketplace might represent. Although large multinationals may get the most attention in the media, the truth is that for virtually any size firm, developing and implementing a sustained growth strategy requires serious consideration be given to moving beyond domestic market boundaries. For a number of reasons, not the least being the internationalization of the marketplace, reliance on a single domestic market is no longer a sustainable long-term business model for the majority of firms. The limited growth opportunities afforded in a single market, coupled with the fact that firms from outside that domestic market are now actively competing for this limited market share, means that small, medium, and large firms must acknowledge the expansion of their operational scope.

Unfortunately, successful international operations demand more than simply expanding a firm's current domestic business model—no matter how successful that model may be, or may have been in the past. The primary key to international success is having a clear understanding of the complex nature of the international business environment. Too often, firms will overlook the knowledge they possess when it comes to operations in their own home market. Having a clear perspective when it comes to elements such as consumer tastes, preferences, and overall behavior as well as product pricing, distribution, and competitive dynamics is crucial for sustaining any business but these pieces of the business environment are frequently second nature when it comes to the firm's domestic market. This is hardly surprising—an established firm must have a clear handle on all of these elements of the environment (and more) to be "established."

However, when these same firms move into new (i.e., international) markets, it is not unusual for them to overlook the need to gain the same level of understanding of all aspects of the environment in this new market. This means carefully considering not only the components of the business environment, but also the various ways in which these could possibly interact, how those interactions may differ from the domestic market, and the impact this will have on current business models and their viability.

Too often any discussion of the international business environment becomes overly focused on cultural differences. Clearly, cultural differences can have a profound effect on the types of products that might appeal to consumers in another market, how those products are used, where they will look for those products, and how to best connect with those consumers. But concentrating too heavily on just cultural differences can result in an incomplete view of an international market for two basic reasons.

First, the business environment comprises many more fundamentally important elements, but this is often overlooked simply because these are considered implicit in strategy development in a domestic market. Put another way, businesses don't ignore the relevant components of their environment when it comes to domestic operations; these components are so interwoven in the strategic process and the development of business models. Further, these components are so familiar that the domestic operational environment is not an unknown quantity. Thus, when a firm moves to an international environment, it is easy to overlook the need to establish a clear picture of the unique environment of this new market. Second, although many firms do not recognize this, it may be that cultural differences are only a small—perhaps even insignificant—characteristic of the international market(s) being considered. Many firms discover that, although cultural differences exist in a market, those differences have little or no impact on their firm or its products.

The overall objective of this book is to provide a clear, practical understanding of the complex nature of the international business environment and its various relevant components. The goal is not to provide a guide to creating and implementing an international strategy. Rather, by carefully considering the complex nature of the international business environment and how its various components may, or may not, affect firm operations, a manager will have a foundation for creating that long-term successful international strategy. To begin, this chapter addresses the complexities of the international business environment but not before discussing two critical elements: why international operations are so important for the 21st-century firm and what firms can expect to achieve by "going international."

The International Business Environment: An Issue of Complexities

So if truly understanding the international business environment means going beyond focusing just on cultural differences, where is the best place to start? The answer is in what makes international business different from domestic operations. Given all the attention directed toward international business as a distinctly unique operational exercise, it is safe to assume that there must be unique aspects associated with international business compared with domestic business. These can be most succinctly described in terms of three issues: 1) the unique aspects of the market environment, 2) the available strategy options, and 3) the different market entry options. Each of these issues represents a real departure from those most commonly associated with domestic operations.

In the case of the first, the unique aspects of the market environment, the crucial point is recognizing the problems of operating in two, or more, markets. The differences encountered in the various marketplaces can be substantial and significant. This is not to say that a domestic market environment is not a complex venue for conducting business. A quick look at the impact of economic changes, or shifting demographic patterns, in the U.S. market shows that just these pieces of the overall environment can have a profound impact on firms operating in the United States. Nor does this suggest that there are additional components added to the international business environment. All the same ingredients—culture, politics, economics, for example—are present in any market. Where the complexity enters the equation is in which of the various market environment components are significant and relevant to a given firm and how these may change from market to market. The reality is simple: market differences exist across markets. The challenge faced by firms is twofold. First, they must have a clear idea of which aspects of the market differ from the market(s) in which they currently operate. Second, they need to ascertain whether these differences have any impact on their particular firm. A theme that will occur over and over as we look at the various facets of the international business environment is that differences do not necessarily require actions—they may have no impact on a given firm at all.

The second issue that makes the international business environment unique involves how the firm will choose to operate in their international markets relative to their domestic market. This is a question of strategy options. Although it is not impossible for a firm to "export" its domestic business model, what is successful in one market can be a complete disaster in another. A truly unique aspect of international business involves being able to manage different business models. Put another way, this second issue is all about coordinating different strategies for different markets. Sometimes this will mean developing a totally different approach for one market compared with another. Other times, it might mean that the best option is for the firm to develop a universal strategy that is "plug-and-play" across multiple markets. Or it is possible, under the right conditions, for a firm to be able to use the same business model that works in their domestic market in other markets internationally. Regardless, the need to consider multiple strategy options rather than automatically relying on what has worked well in the past in the domestic market makes international business, and effectively operating in the international business environment, unique.

The third, and last, issue that makes the international business environment and international business operations unique involves the various market entry options. In a domestic market, the question of how a firm, and its product, will not only physically enter the market but also present itself (i.e., imported, domestic, etc.) is a moot point. The firm is there; the product is there. Entering an international market presents a whole new set of problems in terms of market entry options. The firm must decide how it will move the product into, and through, the market as well as take into account how that strategic choice will affect their overall operational strategy. For example, will the market entry strategy position the firm and its product as an outsider? Sometimes this approach is appropriate— imported products are often perceived as being of higher quality and can therefore demand a higher price. At the same time, the ability to sustain revenues as a high-priced imported good may be problematic if economic instability exists in that market or if there is a high level of negative attitudes toward "foreign" companies and their products.

These issues need to be fully dealt with before any discussion of the actual international business environment can begin. However, that discussion begs two important questions. First, if the international business environment, and operating within it, is so complicated then why bother?

Second, if the firm chooses to operate in this complicated environment what is it trying to achieve? Let's delve deeper into these questions before returning to the issues of what makes the international business environment unique and how best to prepare for dealing with it.

Is Being "International" an Option?

Taking into account the complex nature of the international business environment—and the potential operational problems that a firm might encounter when moving into the global marketplace—the obvious question becomes are international operations really necessary? Put another way: is being "international" an option or a requirement? Although many managers might argue that the U.S. domestic market continues to represent a single market of opportunity, thereby suggesting that international operations are not a requirement in today's business world, the reality is that no firm regardless of size can avoid, whether directly or indirectly, being "international."

In their book *The Quest for Global Dominance*, Gupta, Govindarajan, and Wang (2008) provide a compelling argument that no firm can avoid the international marketplace—that being "international" is not an option. They build their case around "imperatives" and "globalization" characteristics that show that not only are international operations not to be avoided but that by embracing the idea of going international firms large, small, and in-between can better position themselves for long-term success in the ever-challenging modern market. The imperatives are growth, efficiency, and knowledge, and the globalization characteristics involve customers and competitors. To have a true sense of the stage on which the international environment and international operations are based, it is useful to consider each of these carefully.

The Growth Imperative

The so-called Growth Imperative in and of itself may be the single best argument for firms to look outside their domestic marketplace. For firms to continue to succeed over time the ability to grow is paramount. Few companies, no matter how successful, would say that their strategy for the future is to stand pat on their current market share and performance. Long-term, even short-term, success requires increased sales, revenues, market share, and customers. Unfortunately, for those firms committed to only domestic operations—even in a market as substantial as the United States—the opportunity for growth in these areas is increasingly limited.

First, there are the problems and challenges associated with operating in a mature market. The product life cycle can give many clues as to the nature of a market, and how businesses in that market must operate to remain relevant. This product life cycle comprises four basic stages: introductory, growth, maturity, and decline. The introductory stage is when a product is first introduced and profits are generally negative. The goal is to get the market to accept the product. In the growth stage, sales and profits take off, signaling competitors that they should enter the market with similar products. This is the most profitable but also the shortest stage in terms of time. The mature stage—the longest of the four—is when sales and profits begin to level off and the firm is focused on maintaining market share and profits in the face of high levels of competition. The decline stage represents products that the market has determined are no longer relevant with a resulting drop in sales. Firms with products in the mature stage are centered on keeping their products relevant and profitable.

The United States is the classic example of a mature market. For firms in this market, whether they are targeting individual consumers or other businesses, their product and its functions are well established. Further, when new products enter the market they quickly move (assuming they do not fail altogether) from the introductory and growth stages to the maturity stage. This stage is characterized by a wide variety of product choices (read: competitors) and customers who are familiar with their product options.

There are three basic approaches to growing in this type of market environment. The first is to find new customers within the current market environment. This means finding new market segments that, for whatever reason, the firm chose not to target previously. These segments may have been avoided because they were not considered profitable enough in the past or because the product was determined to not be as relevant to that segment(s) as it was to those customer segments already targeted. Either way, the "quality" of these new customers may be questionable. A second option is to find new uses for the product. This too has its potential drawbacks because it may require the product to be adapted, and product adaptations can be expensive. Alternatively, it may mean that the product is now being presented to the market to be used in a way that it was not originally intended. In either case, the costs—whether direct, indirect, or opportunity-based—could be significant. The third option would be to seek out similar customers, using the product in similar ways, in new markets. International markets.

So sustaining growth, based on the characteristics of a mature market, is an issue most U.S. firms must address. There are also the challenges associated with the economy and current economic conditions in the United States. It is beyond the scope of this book to go into the details of the most recent, and ongoing, economic situation in the United States—stagnant growth, high unemployment, government deficits, consumer debt, the list goes on. Any firm planning for growth over the next decade would view the U.S. market with real trepidation. The prospects for U.S.-based corporate growth is not necessarily a positive one for most firms—particularly for those used to the relatively unfettered growth opportunities this market presented in the 1990s on through the early part of the 21st century. Any real sustainable growth will have to come from other markets.

This is not to suggest that other markets have not been similarly affected or that the U.S. economy is an isolated case. European markets are also faced with serious economic challenges—even crises in some countries. It has been said that when the U.S. coughs, Europe catches a cold. The interrelationship of the U.S. economy, the European Union, and individual European countries means that, from the perspective of the economic environment, many of the same problems that plague the United States exist in these other markets—perhaps even more seriously. However, this is not to say there is no opportunity in these markets. Like the United States, which remains a global economic power, the opportunities exist; they may just take different forms. This may mean for some firms that growth can be achieved through continued attention being placed on the United States with additional focus on the European Union. Although less attractive than in years past, the European Union still represents a large, essentially single market in terms of market entry issues and therefore a means through which growth can be maintained at the individual firm level. Furthermore, this movement into Europe would mean both a presence once the economic downturn subsides and also a means of diversifying markets. Finally, many other markets outside of Europe (e.g., China, India) may not have the same economic issues as the United States and Europe, making them another attractive choice for long-term growth.

The Efficiency Imperative

If the Growth Imperative does not provide a compelling enough case for international operations, consider the Efficiency Imperative. Virtually every firm seeks to grow over time. This means increasing sales and revenues through the acquisition of new customers and the expansion into new markets and market segments. However, simply placing the company into such a market setting is not necessarily sufficient. The firm must then be able to succeed in the face of other competitors. This is where the

Efficiency Imperative enters the picture. Businesses that operate across different markets become more efficient as they leverage the unique characteristics of these market environments.

Markets that have opportunities generally have unique strengths and advantages that can create synergies and increase competitive advantage. A common advantage would be lower labor costs, which reduce overall production costs, resulting in higher margins. That is, perhaps, the most commonly recognized advantage associated with international operations. Unfortunately, if this were the only significant efficiency advantage to operating outside of the domestic market then it would be exclusive to manufacturing firms, or those with substantial labor-intensive costs. Although the ability to lower labor costs through offshore manufacturing is a distinct operational advantage, the increased efficiencies that go along with international operations can extend far beyond the cost of production-associated labor.

As the service component of firms' product offerings has increased, many of these firms find increased efficiencies in other markets not simply through inexpensive labor but also in more affordable, highly skilled labor. This means increased efficiencies can be obtained not just through increased labor quantity, based on a finite cost, but also increased quality. Traditionally, the U.S. market was associated with highly educated and highly skilled employees. Although that has not changed, many other markets have raised the standard of their skilled labor force to a level that meets, and sometimes exceeds, that of U.S. employees—and at a much lower cost. For example, a large segment of the population of India are not only highly versed in technology, and technology-related fields, they are also fluent English speakers. Furthermore, what is considered to be a decent middle-class income in India would be a fraction of what a comparable engineer, programmer, or information systems professional would require in the United States. Thus, if a firm that provides technical support to its customers can pay qualified support staff, say, 25 percent of what similar domestic-based employees would be paid, serious efficiencies can be realized, making the firm more competitive.

These efficiencies are not limited just to labor advantages, whether quantity or quality. They also extend to other operational advantages. Advantages associated with location (e.g., proximity to inputs or new customer segments), production synergies (e.g., product design expertise), market knowledge, and operational efficiencies can be realized when a firm has multiple market environments in which to conduct business. The Growth Imperative recognizes the need for companies to grow, and the means through which this can be accomplished via international operations. The

Efficiency Imperative recognizes that international operations do not represent just additional operational costs; the distinct characteristics of each market may mean that by leveraging these characteristics, the firm may be able to become more efficient.

The Knowledge Imperative

The third imperative—Knowledge—recognizes that the Efficiency Imperative can be used to take the firm yet another step further. Whereas the Efficiency Imperative is all about leveraging market and location advantages to increase operational efficiency, the Knowledge Imperative is about applying lessons learned in one market to gain, or regain, competitive advantages in other markets. Put another way, the unique requirements of one local market may be "exportable" to other markets to create competitive advantage in multiple markets.

Regardless of the global nature of the marketplace, differences across markets persist. Consumers have different tastes and preferences, use products for different purposes, use varying amounts, and may place emphasis on different aspects of value that the product represents. Similarly, the business customer may apply different criteria in purchasing and using a product. However, firms operating across different markets often discover that product characteristics sought by customers in one market may, for related but not necessarily identical reasons, seek out similar product characteristics and respond to the same "reasons to buy" a product.

A good illustration of the Knowledge Imperative in action would be the example of the changes made to disposable diapers for Asian markets and how those changes were then "exported" back to the U.S. manufacturers of disposable diapers, which originally had the best-performing products available. Unfortunately, for all but one of these manufacturers, the U.S. domestic market was dominated by a single brand. That left the second place firm in a competitive bind. Under the existing market conditions, it was unlikely that the company's brand would be able to make substantial inroads in terms of additional market share. Thus, the Growth Imperative drove the firm to seek out other nondomestic markets. Asian markets were determined to be particularly attractive given the cultural importance placed on children—and the resulting money spent—along with the fact that the disposable diapers in those markets were generally inferior compared with the U.S. product. However, living space and storage constraints meant that for the U.S. product to serve the needs of the market, the product had to be adapted so that it performed (dryness, absorbency, etc.) at the same high level but was made so that each diaper was significantly smaller (i.e., easier to store). Developing a batting material that met these requirements was accomplished, and the firm was able to grow revenues through its Asian markets rather than relying on the U.S. domestic market.

The Knowledge Imperative then enters the equation. Changes in the U.S. market made the appeal of easier-to-store diapers a product characteristic that American consumers now began to seek out. The issue was not limited to storage at home. The demand for these new diapers were related to demographic changes in the United States—most specifically, the increase in two-income families and the subsequent rise in day care and young children being frequently transported outside of the home. In short, U.S. families did not necessarily have the same storage challenges in their home as the Asian families, but young children on the move need diaper bags not cupboards. All else being equal, the more diapers that could be stored in the diaper bag the more that particular brand would appeal to U.S. parents. Recognition of this subtle, but important, shift in consumer needs meant that the firm that had "learned" how to meet this need in the Asian countries was able to apply that knowledge back in their domestic market with the end result being an increase in market share in the United States.

Like the Efficiency Imperative, the Knowledge Imperative is all about recognizing that international operations are more than just costs and revenues to be balanced out over each market in which the firm operates. The truly international firm understands that by operating in other markets, there may be efficiencies and knowledge that can be leveraged in other markets which, in turn, create competitive advantages. Each of the three imperatives discussed represent compelling reasons for firms of any size not only to consider the opportunities that international operations present but also the advantages that competing firms may have over firms that choose not to engage in operations outside of their domestic market. The two "globalization" aspects of the international business environment show how the new face of customers and competitors make it impossible for any business to view itself solely as a domestic firm.

The Globalization of Customers

In some sense, it could be argued that the three imperatives just discussed form the basis for the dynamic nature of the international business environment. That is, the Growth, Efficiency, and Knowledge Imperatives create the stage for the distinguishing characteristics of the 21st-century global marketplace. The globalization of customers, and competitors, looks at the two other primary participants in the international business environment. The first, understanding the global nature of customers around the world—both in domestic and international markets—is crucial for corporate sustainability and growth. The second, understanding the globalization of competitors, influences the firm's ability to operate at maximum efficiency in all marketplaces.

The globalization of customers refers to the fact that, as more firms move into more markets around the world, customers will be exposed to a larger number of product choices. This changes the consumer environment in a number of ways—enough material for a book covering just global consumer behavior. However, for this discussion, which is designed to develop an understanding of the issues faced by firms attempting to navigate the international business environment, understanding two issues related to these global customers becomes paramount. First, having an ever-increasing number of product choices has helped to undermine the whole concept of brand loyalty. Second, this increased product selection—coupled with other changes such as the increase in information available to consumers—means that companies must be prepared for customers who are informed.

The challenge presented by consumers who are more and more comfortable with a wide range of product choices is a double-edged sword. On one hand, consumers with more product choices from a large number of both domestic and international companies means that they are more easily lured from one product or brand to another. This means that it is easier than it has been previously for firms new to a market to successfully entice consumers to purchase a new and different product. Consumer behavior in the 21st century international business environment has shown that firms can make tremendous headway in markets wherein it would have previously been difficult to achieve even modest success.

A case in point is the Korean car manufacturer Hyundai. The stated goal of the firm a few years back was to have a greater percentage of market share in the United States than Toyota had. Conventional wisdom said such a goal was unattainable, especially considering the long and established presence enjoyed by Toyota in the United States. However, after only a few years, the results speak for themselves. Although Hyundai has not supplanted any of the Japanese automakers in the American market, it has made significant strides in that direction. Much of this has to do with the level of comfort U.S. consumers have with a large number of product choices from firms around the globe when it comes to buying a car. Unfortunately, this cuts both ways because those same consumers would have little reluctance to move to another brand if the buying proposition was appealing—those customers who are now buying Korean cars were obviously buying something else at some point in time.

The second potential problem that these globalized customers represent is a natural result of having more products from which to choose. In making product choices, consumers naturally seek out information to facilitate that decision-making process. As the number of the potential choices increases, so does the amount of information that must be gathered. This means that the consumer of the 21st century is comfortable dealing with product information. The knowledge serves to make it easier to select the best product when many are faced with reduced economic resources. For firms, an informed consumer is desirable. At the same time, having informed consumers also means they are more demanding given that they not only know what other alternative products *have* to offer, they establish higher expectations of any individual product given that they know what the best products actually *can* offer. In short, the global consumer is open to new firms and their products, but having these individuals purchase the product does not mean the firm has captured and held market share.

The Globalization of Competitors

The final piece in this "to be, or not to be" internationalization discussion is the globalized nature of a firm's competition. Because *all* firms seek to increase sales and revenues, any given company, regardless of size, can anticipate being placed in a situation in which, regardless of their own operational scope, they are international. Even the smallest local firm can find itself competing with nondomestic firms. For example, a small local specialty-grocery store could easily be threatened by the availability of similar products through online ordering. Firms that build a premium-pricing strategy around customer service may find their market share eroded due to competitor's lower prices achieved through the economies of scale that can accompany increasing the number of markets in which they operate. The possibility of similar situations is endless.

Irrespective of the scenario, the bottom line is this: all firms face the same pressures and opportunities when it comes to international operations and, although an individual firm may opt out of direct international operations, at least some portion of their competing firms will be from other markets. So if international business, at some level, is unavoidable, what can firms expect to achieve when they enter this complex market environment? The key to success is for the firm to have a clear idea going into international operations exactly what it is trying to achieve. There are several reasonable overall objectives that firms can attempt to achieve, but trying to do too much can result in a confused strategy and, potentially, failure in the firm's international efforts.

International Business Objectives

There are four categories of objectives typically associated with international operations: increased sales/revenue, the acquisition of resources, the diversification of sales and/or suppliers, and minimizing competitive risk. Each set represents reasonable goals for any firm to seek to achieve. However, each requires substantial resources and because of these costs may not necessarily be mutually supportive. The best way for a firm to succeed in finding the way through the complex international business environment is to first have a clear and defined notion of exactly what its goals are in operating outside of the familiar confines of the domestic market.

Increased Sales and Revenues: Environment Differences Increase Opportunity

The most obvious goal for international operations is to directly increase the firm's profits. However, simply selling a product in a new market does not guarantee success—even if there appear to be no clear competing products in that market. Typically, the firm that seeks to quickly increase sales and revenue by moving into a nondomestic market, or markets, will likely be most successful when it looks for one of three types of markets: those with pent-up latent demand, those with cultural characteristics that will facilitate relatively high levels of product usage, and those with favorable product life cycle differences compared with the domestic market.

When a country begins to move through the phases of economic and market development, latent consumer demand begins to become evident. This latent demand is caused by a lack of products in that market and fueled, through the globalization of consumer information, so that as the economy is better able to support the sales of a wide range of consumer goods and services the lack of these over time means that demand can easily outstrip supply. Further, given that these countries are newly developing, there is a lack of domestic market producers for consumer products. In the past two decades, China is a prime example of an economy in which, regardless of domestic development, demand has far outstripped the ability of the market to supply the products sought by the country's newly empowered consumers. Such a situation, even in a highly regulated economy such as China, means that for non-Chinese firms—especially those providing consumer products—there have been, and continue to be, substantial opportunities to generate increased levels of sales and revenues.

Cultural differences across domestic and nondomestic markets can also create opportunities to quickly increase profits. These cultural differences can mean that a culturally based sales cycle can be mitigated. For example, generally the peak times for U.S. retailers—and the products they sell—are the run-up to Christmas and the August back-to-school timeframe. For many of these stores, and the producers of their products, the time in between (particularly the first three months of the year) can represent slow sales. Some of these firms have discovered that other cultures—Asian cultures in particular—have gift-giving seasons that offset the retail sales valleys experienced in the United States. Thus, these cultural differences can not only increase sales but also help to provide a more steady revenue stream. Another potentially favorable cultural difference that can increase sales is a cultural propensity to consume more of the product than the domestic market. Here a good example would be U.S. rice growers who recognize that although their product may be consumed irregularly by American consumers, it is consumed several times a day in Asia.

Lastly, product life cycle differences can create an environment favorable for increasing sales and revenues. This situation occurs when a product, or some variation of the product, moves "back" in the product life cycle when it enters a new market. The problem of products in the mature stage of the product life cycle has been discussed previously. When a firm can take its existing product to a market where it is not as well known, or as widely used, it can in effect become a "new" product—with all the attending sales and revenue advantages associated with the growth stage of the product life cycle. Apple's ability to adapt the iPod technology to meet the demands of this type of market, such as the iPod Shuffle, demonstrates how a product can continue to generate new sales long after it has reached the mature stage in its domestic market.

Acquire Resources—Environment Differences Increase Competitiveness

A second, equally reasonable but perhaps less obvious, objective of a firm's international operations would be to acquire resources from nondomestic markets that, in turn, would enable the firm to be more efficient—and by extension more profitable—in all markets. This approach could easily be viewed strictly from the perspective of gaining access to raw materials or other physical production inputs, but to view international resource acquisition only from that perspective would be unnecessarily restrictive. Certainly, acquiring physical resources may be an important motivating factor for moving outside of the comfort of a domestic market, but a firm could be just as equally motivated by the prospect of acquiring intellectual or financial resources.

History has shown that obtaining physical inputs has been viewed as a political justification for entering other markets—sometimes through the use of military force such as the expansion of the Japanese empire, which precipitated the war in China and the Pacific during the 1930s and 1940s. Fortunately, firm-level initiatives to gain these physical resources from nondomestic sources are generally less dramatic. At the individual corporate level, the two basic types of physical resources sought for are labor and production inputs (e.g., raw materials, component parts).

Labor can come in many forms ranging from inexpensive manual or semimanual, manufacturing workers up through educated employees with higher-level technical skills and knowledge. The latter is better placed in a discussion of intellectual and knowledge resources, but the notion that other markets can be a good source of inexpensive production-oriented labor is reasonable. Goodyear Tire & Rubber Company, which accounts for upward of 40 percent of all tire production in the world, has found that tapping into the Asian labor market enables the firm to maintain a higher level of global competitiveness through less expensive production labor costs. The fact that the tires manufactured in Asian plants can be exported throughout the world more cheaply than if the same tires were produced in the target country where labor costs (e.g., local labor unions and the associated costs) are prohibitively high provides ample evidence for the value of international resource acquisition. Similarly, the concentrated abundance of production inputs such as raw materials or components in a particular location can create economies of scale that can be leveraged across multiple operational locations.

Where physical resources are more commonly associated with manufacturing firms, the acquisition of intellectual or knowledge resources can be an advantage for firms of all types. As was discussed previously in this chapter (see the "Knowledge Imperative" section), the nature of the global marketplace is such that operating in multiple markets can result in the ability to use what the firm might learn in one market in others as well. Although related, the acquisition of intellectual or knowledge resources is somewhat different. Companies that seek to acquire intellectual resources desire to use the special knowledge in a particular market to improve overall operational effectiveness. For example, the Ford Motor Company's long-term close relationship with Mazda was built around the recognition, on the part of Ford, that Mazda had special knowledge in the area of engine building, which enhanced Ford's overall operations.

A third category of resource acquisition would be financial resources. Similar to the goal of increasing sales or revenues, firms that seek to acquire financial resources through international operations often do so with the intent of using those additional funds to maintain, or increase, competitiveness in another market(s). McDonald's Corporation effectively employed this strategy in the early part of this century. The high level of profitability in other markets—especially Asia and Europe—meant that the company had financial resources to invest in rebuilding the firm's product offering in the United States. This ultimately resulted in the firm experiencing healthy growth at the same time its largest domestic competitor (i.e., Burger King) was experiencing almost exactly the same level of sales decline.

Diversify Sales and Suppliers—More Markets Spread Risks

A third objective for firms involved in international business would be diversification within the supply and value chain. The goal firms seek to accomplish using this approach involves risk reduction through market diversification. This risk reduction can be targeted at any, or all, of the three pieces of the microeconomic, or industry, environment—namely, customers, competitors, or suppliers.

Moving into other market can enable firms to offset sales fluctuations (e.g., seasonal or cyclical) by spreading out the company's customer base. A U.S. firm that has a seasonal product, such as apparel, could offset seasonal sales fluctuations by entering markets in the Southern Hemisphere where the climate seasons are the opposite of the home market. At the same time, a firm could also reduce the impact of its prime competitors by seeking out markets where that competitor may not have as strong a brand name or as much market share—which is exactly the motivation behind Pepsi's decision to enter the Eastern European markets as part of their worldwide battle against Coca-Cola. A firm could also use multiple-market operations to reduce supplier dependency while increasing efficiencies because local suppliers not only can be a key factor in international supply chain effectiveness, but having multiple suppliers places the firm in a position in which it is not bound to the fortunes of another company.

Minimize Competitive Risk—Knowing the "Enemy"

The fourth, and final, international business objective set by firms could be the goal of minimizing competitive risk. The discussion of the Efficiency and Knowledge Imperatives shows that firms can realize significant gains through the information and skills obtained when operating in nondomestic markets. These gains can easily result in gathering knowledge that converts directly into competitive advantage. These international operations can also be used to gain competitive advantage through the leveraging of potential corporate synergies—such as brand equity that may extend across market boundaries—providing additional resources that can be used to reduce competitive threats. International operations can also be employed as a means of mitigating the impact of the market power, or market share, of strong local and regional competitors.

Regardless of the set of objectives selected by a firm for its involvement in the global marketplace, it is essential for that firm to have a clear, well-defined set of objectives that do not interfere or contradict one another. The most effective firms are those that do not try to accomplish too much, especially when they are new to international business. The drivers, or imperatives, for international operations are clear, but so are the complexities of the international business environment. Assuming that international business is "the same thing, only different" compared with domestic operations can be a recipe for failure. Before tackling the complexities of the international business environment—assuming the firm accepts that some level of international activity or exposure is unavoidable—a corporate direction that establishes an understanding of what is desired from international operations is the key first step to understanding the global marketplace. From there, the firm can face the complexities and choices that are the hallmarks of the international business environment.

What Makes the International Business Environment Unique ... Revisited

Challenges in the Business Environment

As we look forward to our discussion of the global marketplace and its environment, it is important to establish one clear fact: the components that comprise this international business environment are not different from those that form the domestic market. The pieces—social/cultural, physical/geographic, political/legal, economic, competitive, technological, and so on—remain unchanged. What does change, however, is the impact each may have on international business and how, from market to market, that impact can vary across the various components of the given business environment. Under these circumstances, the problem faced by businesses is this: the right approach to dealing with one market—and its corresponding environment—will not necessarily transfer to any other market. Put another way, although the variables remain the same across markets, the equation for success will likely change. As noted at the beginning of this chapter, this is the first thing that makes operating in the international business environment unique.

The impact each of the key areas of the international business environment has on firm operations varies. At some level, it is correct to assume that this impact universally leads to increased risks, but the nature of this heightened risk, and indeed whether it applies to any given firm, can cause any business to see the environment differently from others operating in that same market. For example, a firm like FedEx may see the primary risk factors in the physical/geographic component of the environment (e.g., effects on response time, damages to shipped goods) and the political/legal environment (e.g., laws and regulations that address what can be shipped and how). Alternatively, a firm such as Subway would potentially view the primary risk factors to be cultural/social (e.g., food tastes and preferences), economic (e.g., stability of demand, ability to pay), and local competitive forces.

Regardless of the composition of the international business environment in which a firm operates, the most effective and efficient firms do not immediately adopt an operational attitude that centers on altering its business model to fit the threats, real and perceived, that might exist in that environment. A key theme throughout this book is that, for long-term success, firms recognize the need to participate in actively, and attempt to manage, their international business operational environment. The firms that are truly successful over time tend to be those that have an approach to the global marketplace identified as "directive" rather than "adaptive."

A firm with a directive perspective on the international business environment views the environment in which it operates being, to some degree, controllable. Classic business theory is built around the notion that the business environment, whether domestic or international, is essentially uncontrollable. By extension, any firm faced with a threat would need to adapt its operations and business model to accommodate that threat. The adaptive firm concludes that the business environment is uncontrollable, which means the environment represents restrictions around which the firm must conform if it is to operate at some level of success. The directive firm does not accept this approach—at least not initially. The directive firm approaches the international business environment with the attitude that any risks or threats in that market should be managed rather than simply conformed to. These firms take an initial approach that assumes that threatening aspects of the international environment can be somehow reduced, removed, or transposed by efforts on the part of the firm.

That is not to imply that all risks and threats associated with the international business environment can be controlled at the firm level. However, by proactively considering how these challenges can be managed, rather than adapted to, the directive firm adopts a strategic mind-set that is proactive—and by extension more likely to place the firm in a superior competitive position. One of the most important underlying themes of this book is that the successful firm not only understands the global market-place and all the attending market environments, but it also actively participates in its markets of operations in order to achieve maximum results.

If some firms operate as "adaptives" and others are "directives," the question then becomes: what leads a firm to be directive? The answer is multifaceted. First, firms inclined toward being directive are those that, first and foremost, consider the issue at hand to represent a substantial threat. This seems intuitive, but a truly directive firm devotes substantial resources to monitoring its operational environment so that it can sort out the real threats from the perceived threats. One of the most common errors firms make when operating internationally is to assume that environmental differences represent substantial operational threats. Cultural differences, for example, may exist—and they may represent some level of threat. However, that threat may not be substantial enough to have an impact on the firm's potential for success. McDonald's is generally not viewed positively from the perspective of French consumers, yet the attractiveness of the restaurants and the menu offering means that, irrespective of what the French might think of McDonald's in general terms, the firm has achieved serious growth in France over the past several years. A directive firm has a firm grasp of its international business environment and knows when proactive actions are appropriate.

Directive firms also recognize the need to gain competitive advantage from these "directive" efforts. Because of the resources involved in proactive participation in any business environment, the best firms will only engage in these activities if the end result is to gain advantage over other firms in the market. A company may move to have its products reclassified to avoid a tariff but will only do so if the result is likely to lead either to an increase in market share or the ability to reposition the product in such a way as to avoid its present set of competitors. Along the same lines, the directive firm will see a favorable cost-benefit coming from its efforts. There is no need to engage the threatening component of the environment if it will require more resources than can be gained.

The last driver that should lead a firm to consider whether being directive is an appropriate course of action would be the ethical ramifications of its choice. Managing, or somehow altering, the environment in which the firm operates is not a process performed in a vacuum. These actions have the potential to have an impact on customers, other firms, even the market in general. The history of international business over the years is littered with examples of firms whose actions—ranging from damage to the natural environment all the way to sponsoring assassinations—were motivated by a drive for success that led to what are clearly unethical decisions.

The truly successful international firm recognizes that its actions in its market(s) of operations will have consequences which may not be positive and that must be controlled. The long-term successful international business is one with high ethical standards.

Strategy Options

One of the most difficult operational issues a firm moving into the global marketplace faces is the need to reconcile its domestic and international operations. Taking into account the distinct features of the market environment in which the firm has chosen to operate, it has three basic strategy options: a domestic extension strategy, a multidomestic strategy, and a global strategy. Depending on the goals of the firm and the market(s) selected, each of these strategy options can be viable and appropriate. However, the complexity of the firm's overall international business environment will help to dictate which would best fit its proposed business model. Having a clear and accurate understanding of the business environment within each and every market the firm operates, or proposes to operate in, will help to select the best possible strategy option.

A domestic extension strategy is one in which the firm chooses to adopt the same business model, based on the domestic marketing mix (i.e., price, product, place, and promotion) across all international markets. This means the firm will present those markets with a product essentially unchanged, to the same target market(s), at the same price, connecting with customers using the same promotion activities. This is a quick and relatively inexpensive means of engaging in international operations, but to be effective, one particular assumption must hold. The success of a domestic extension strategy is predicated on the fact that no significant differences exist in the selected international business environment(s) when compared with the firm's domestic market—at least in terms of the firm's own individual product offering. To be successful, this characteristic of the firm's international business environment must be in place.

On the other end of the spectrum is the multidomestic strategy. Whereas the domestic extension strategy assumes little or no differences exist between the domestic market environment and the targeted international markets, the multidomestic strategy assumes that any identified differences in the business environment are substantial enough to warrant the development of an individual business plan for each individual market. The creation of a distinct strategy and marketing mix for each market in which the firm operates is typically only used when the firm can identify one market, or a limited number of markets, that represent huge opportunities, due to the large amount of resources required to create market-specific business models. In a multidomestic scenario, the end result will be independent strategies for each market in which the firm operates based on the market's unique business environment. For example, in the domestic market, the firm's product may be the accepted low-price, low-quality choice, but in an international market virtually the same product can be positioned as a premium-priced import. The most important driver associated with choosing a multidomestic strategy is the business environment of the given international market.

Last, is the global strategy option. The firm that adopts a global strategy essentially lumps all business models together—domestic and international—and seeks to standardize wherever and whenever possible, only making alterations in this universal operational approach when the specific characteristics of a market environment demands. This global strategy option is best characterized by the phrase "think global, act local." For example, McDonald's has constructed its global strategy around what the company says all consumers around the world want from McDonald's: value, service, and quality. Using these basic strategy building blocks, McDonald's then "interprets" them in each individual market in which the firm operates. Provided a company can correctly identify the basic strategy components on which to build this global approach, the advantages are clear: cost savings through economies of scale, a consistent product offering, and synergistic market segmentation strategies. These generally offset the potential of opportunity costs associated with a "compromise" strategy and the problem of knowing exactly when and where standardization is possible and "acting local" necessary.

Market Entry Options

The last piece that sets international business—and operating in an international environment—apart from domestic operations is the various market entry options. Although this book deals with the various aspects of the international business environment, the impact of the environment on a firm is, to some extent, determined by the firm's choice of market entry. There are three basic means through which a firm can enter a nondomestic market: exporting, some form of partnership, or foreign direct investment (FDI). These can be used to mitigate risk factors in a market environment because they enable the firm to control the amount of exposure to market risk.

Exporting, often characterized as "build it here, sell it there," involves keeping as many assets and proprietary resources in the firm's home market as possible, thereby reducing many of the threats associated with operating internationally. However, this approach to a new market can also limit opportunities because the firm will find itself somewhat removed from that market which, in turn, reduces its knowledge of the market. Partnerships with local firms can provide essential market knowledge and access to customers through established distribution channels, but they can increase firm exposure to the risks of "sharing" assets and proprietary resources with that local firm. Foreign direct investment overcomes both the problem of being removed from the market and sharing with a partner, but the biggest risk factor here would be the commitment of high levels of resources to the new nondomestic market.

By placing the challenges of international operations—the complex business environment, strategy choices, and market entry options—into the larger context of globalization and the objectives sought by international firms, we are now in a position to delve more deeply into the various aspects of the international business environment and understand exactly how each has the potential to influence the success, or failure, of a company's international initiatives.

The Firm and the International Business Environment

As we move forward and begin to consider the various components of the international business environment in greater depth, some basic assumptions are implicit in all of our discussion. The first may seem obvious but bears consideration: all firms want to succeed in their international operations. The theme of this book is that the successful firm will actively assess, analyze, and where appropriate manage, its international business environment rather than simply attempting to "export" its domestic business model and hope for the best. Another assumption we will make is that all firms seek to gain competitive advantage. It is simply not enough to maintain a steady level of revenue and market share; the truly successful firm will want to win, not just exist in its international market(s).

Third, we will assume that, depending on the nature of any given international market and its business environment, that different types of resources may be required in order to be effectively proactive and all firms have limited resources. Further, we will assume that resources will only be deployed by the firm to manage the environment when there is some cost benefit. Taken together, these two assumptions recognize the need to consider carefully all aspects of the market environment and only act on issues that represent real threats and that can also be effectively dealt with. Finally, we will assume that managers can perceive any given business environment differently resulting in different responses. This means that rather than seeking a definitive, "correct" response to challenges in the international business environment, the best managers will not be afraid to make a timely, but informed, decision.

Summary

In this chapter, we have discussed what makes operating in the international business environment unique—the challenges of dealing with the various components of that environment and their complex interrelationships as well as the strategy options and market entry choices which also face the firm. We have also put the whole notion of international operations into the larger context of globalization and the objectives firms seek to realize in their international activities. Operating successfully in an international market requires more than coming to terms with cultural differences. The complexities of the various components of the market environment must be fully explored, operational objectives clearly defined, strategy options closely considered, and the appropriate market entry strategy determined. Underlying all of this are the "drivers" of globalization, which make international business, at some level, a reality for all firms. Understanding the pieces of the international business environment means first understanding its operational context.

CHAPTER TWO

Dealing with the Social and Cultural Aspects of a New Market

Introduction

In the previous chapter, we discussed that understanding the international business environment means so much more than just observing, and acting on, cultural differences. That being said, we start our deeper exploration of the international business environment with the cultural and social aspects of a new market. The social and cultural aspects of global operations is a natural starting point not just because it may be the most obvious point of departure when comparing domestic and international business. More important, the social and cultural environments deal directly with the basic building blocks of any business and its operations—people. Society, and the social environment, involves human interaction, and culture is the foundation for these interactions. Business simply does not exist as a functioning activity without individuals operating within the organization and those individuals, in turn, interfacing with other people—competitors, suppliers and partner firms, and customers—on the outside. In this chapter, we consider what culture is from the perspective of the firm, its different "ingredients," how the firm can view cultural differences in terms of dealing with its competition, and how to address cultural differences both within the organization as well as in the larger outside market.

What "Culture" Is—and What It Is Not

Coming to grips with "culture," from an international business perspective, is best approached through a definition that is business oriented. Culture is a multidisciplinary topic spanning sociology, anthropology, psychology, and other areas of social science along with its importance to business—especially international business. Because of this, numerous definitions of "culture" exist, but not all address the key elements of culture that are important for business to understand. The best working definition of culture for business has evolved over time as the impact of culture on business, and vice versa, has become better understood. The first, functional definition of culture for business is based on Herskovits's 1948 foundational statement that culture is "the man-made part of the human environment." Although many other definitions have been put forth, the key element that makes this a good starting place is the term "manmade." This recognizes two important characteristics that have a direct impact on business: 1) that culture is dynamic and 2) that, being "manmade," it can be influenced and shaped. This means that, at its core, culture is not a static barrier but an element that helps construct a society using a process within which business—as a manmade institution—can participate and influence.

Gert Hofstede (1983) adds a second important element in his definition. Hofstede suggested that culture is "the collective programming of the mind which distinguishes the members of one human group from another." Where Herskovits suggests that dynamic and process-oriented nature of culture, Hofstede introduces the notion of "collective programming." Where social scientists are concerned with the nuances of individual beliefs and behaviors, businesses must focus on group behavior. The importance of Hofstede's perspective for international business is this idea of "collective programming"—that is, the recognition that culture binds individuals together into groups who respond and react similarly, thus enabling a firm to develop programs to reach profitable market segments.

These two important notions have resulted in a common definition designed to fit the purposes of businesses in their attempt to better understand what culture is and what it means in terms of firm operations in another market. The definition of culture that seems to best fit the needs of international business is this: all learned behavior shared by a society. Although perhaps not comprehensive enough from a social science point of view, this definition hits the key elements of culture that every business, and business decision maker, should know. Culture is learned, shared, and enforced. This means that if culture is learned, it can be taught. In the information-heavy environment in which people around the world live, there are numerous sources beyond the traditional family unit that provide cues as to how individuals are supposed to act and respond. Many of these information sources are—directly or indirectly—associated with companies and their products. This means that firms can become actively involved in the dynamic process of molding and influencing culture to its own benefit.

The second important element is the idea that culture is shared. Closely related to Hofstede's "collective programming" concept, this recognizes that being able to deal effectively with a different culture means focusing on similarities, rather than differences. It is all too easy to divide groups of people—and it is counterproductive as well. To be successful, firms need substantial markets and target market segments. Identifying characteristics of a culture that are shared across the individual members means that the firm has a set of values and beliefs that are common to the larger group. These form the foundation for business strategies designed to reach whole market segments. One of the basic principles of target marketing is that the selected segments be substantial enough to generate revenue. Focusing on these similarities within an international market helps to ensure sufficiently sizable segments will be identified and acted on.

Last, culture is enforced. All human beings have a need to belong to a group. The value, beliefs, and "learned behavior" that define any given culture form the basis for group membership. This means that once these learned behaviors have been adopted within a culture, they must be adhered to for individuals to remain part of the group. Therefore, a business that can correctly identify cultural characteristics can be reasonably confident that any strategies or tactics built around there characteristics will have a good chance of success.

Understanding these three key elements is crucial for a firm to be able to view culture, and cultural differences, as something other than a nebulous threat. This means recognizing that culture is a system of shared meanings—intangible, perceptual, subjective, and in need of interpretation. It is learned, which means culture can be taught—a process in which firms can participate—and it is dynamic. Finally cultural beliefs and values are group, not individual, oriented and enforced through group membership. Understanding culture, from the perspective of international business, is not about what is right or wrong within that culture. It is dangerous for a business, or its managers, to allow their own cultural values to cloud their judgment in another cultural environment. At best this can create a disconnect within that environment; at worst it could result in the firm and its products being alienated from the very customers it hoped to reach. Culture is not inherited; rather, it is learned and interpreted over time and across age—and other—cohort groups. Finally, it is important to approach culture from the viewpoint of group, not individual values where the focus is on macro characteristics that have an impact on your firm and product, not individual differences. The next step in coming to grips with the culture in this discussion of the international business environment is to consider how culture, and this "learned behavior" that is "shared by a society," may be constructed.

The Ingredients of Culture: Understanding Its Composition

On the surface, trying to analyze another culture from a business perspective seems a daunting task. It is one thing to come to terms with the notion that different cultures have different values, beliefs, and learned behaviors; it is another challenge entirely to find a means to make sense of these differences, or potential differences. In the context of the international business environment, perhaps the best approach to identifying relevant cultural differences is to begin by considering the different types of values, beliefs, and learned behaviors and how these might influence the overall business environment in the specified market. These "types" of differences are best characterized as the "ingredients" of culture and fall into one of five categories: material, social, natural world, aesthetics, and language. Understanding the cultural mix—or the relative high/low importance placed on each of these ingredients in a given culture—enables a firm not only to create effective programs for connecting with customers in a new cultural environment, it also provides guidance for managing employees within that culture as well as help in gaining competitive advantage.

Material Culture

Of all the ingredients of culture, the material aspect is probably the easiest for Americans, and American firms, to grasp. Material culture refers to values and meanings—and the importance placed on these—related to the tangible. For international business, this would refer to a large degree to the extent to which any given culture emphasized possessions. As more attention is focused on obtaining possessions, often in the form of products, the actions of individuals in that culture line up with the goal of business—to provide products that will fulfill the needs of the material aspects of culture. In short, a materially focused culture is one in which a great deal of emphasis is placed on having "stuff." Or alternatively, in a material culture, a person is what he or she owns. Although this might sound extreme, briefly considering how American culture operates shows the importance placed on the material ingredient of culture. Just one example is the fixation on brand names—to the point that Americans will pay to wear items of apparel that are essentially advertisements (e.g., Adidas and Nike T-shirts).

It is relatively easy for U.S. companies to operate in a materially focused culture for two reasons. First, this cultural mind-set closely resembles that of the United States, and second, individuals in these material cultures seek out products—particularly goods, or tangible products—to better fit in that culture. Thus, the firm is in a position to provide something that these consumers are already actively seeking. The only question is how to identify cultures that are materially oriented. This is also not difficult as the cues and clues to the importance placed on "stuff" are readily observable. Markets in which mass promotion such as advertising, in all forms, permeates the society, where there is a heavy emphasis on brands and branding, and where there are deep product lines for consumer goods (e.g., grocery products such as snack foods that are not necessities) all provide clear and obvious indications that the consumers in a market place some degree of importance on the material component of culture. Although on the surface, there might be clear differences in another culture, the fact that it is materially oriented may make the culture, and its members, much more similar for the purposes of a firm and its product(s) than first impressions might indicate.

Social Culture

Whereas a material culture is one that is relatively easy for American firms to understand, the polar opposite—a socially oriented culture—is not. A culture that emphasizes the social ingredient of culture is one that places high levels of importance on values and meanings related to the intangible—most specifically, human interactions. Where firms can generally adapt to a cultural environment that is programmed to focus actively on acquiring products, an environment more inclined toward human social interaction is not one that naturally plays to the product offerings of most companies. Success in a cultural environment with a heavy social emphasis can be a challenge for the business more comfortable with a materially oriented culture, but it is not impossible.

A materially focused cultural environment can be readily identified through obvious market, and marketing, clues such as advertising, branding, and product type/selection. Identifying a social culture involves close observation—not of simple market activities and interactions but of person to person interactions. These observations do not necessarily require knowledge of the language but rather a sense of what to observe both at the individual and group level. In terms of individual interactions, one would look for the frequency and type of touch/contact behavior exhibited between two people in public interactions. Behavior that goes beyond a simple handshake (e.g., opening a meeting with a hug or some form of kiss) and then continues—hand or arm touching, close proximity, and so forth—are all good initial indicators of a sense of social culture. Moving within society in larger groups—for example, family units rather than as individuals, as well as the number and popularity of group activities are good indicators as well.

Once the relatively high importance of the social ingredient of culture can be determined in a given cultural environment, the question then remains: what needs to be done to ensure firm and product success? Product for product's sake is probably not the best approach in this circumstance. Instead, focusing on product features and characteristics—presented in a social rather than a material context—is likely the best approach. One means of accomplishing this might be, for example, emphasizing the safety and product quality of a premium imported product rather than its brand. Such a social responsibility type appeal suggests that purchasing the product in question is good for the consumer *and* all those who may have either indirect or direct contact with the product—and by extension the firm who sells the product. Companies with a specific product to market cannot realistically change their product and business model completely to suit a socially oriented market. However, they can "repackage" what they have to offer, and what their firm does, in that market to be perceived as having a more socially acceptable offerings.

The Natural World

Understanding the importance placed on the natural world in another cultural environment involves understanding the role of values and meanings related to human–spiritual interactions. It is essential at the outset to keep in mind that this particular ingredient of culture is not, strictly speaking, related to a Western sense of religion. Certainly, this part of the cultural environment is where religious aspects of a culture's values are placed. However, to make this element synonymous with "religion" leads to an incomplete, and potentially misleading, sense of the cultural environment being studied. Reducing this discussion of the natural world to the importance of religion in a culture means overlooking the role those values, involving "placing" individuals into some context relative to the world around them and the future, play, thus making an understanding of that culture's broader worldview problematic.

Rather than a focus on religion, coming to terms with this ingredient of culture is more about understanding the role values related to contextualizing the human experience play in a culture. For example, in the United States it would be easy to come to the conclusion that this natural world perspective is not important; after all one of the hallmarks of American culture is supposed to be a clear separation of church and state. However, a key element of American culture is individual rights and freedoms that can be traced directly back to the Puritans who originally colonized America and their religious belief related to individual choice and eternity. A more constructive approach would be to evaluate the cultural environment in terms of the extent to which values related to where humans fit in to the world around them—current and future—are deemed important.

A good starting point in making any determinations regarding the role of the natural world in a given cultural environment would be to consider how the culture places humans within the context of the greater world around them; is the culture primarily vertical/hierarchical or horizontal/parallel. Judeo-Christian Western culture is predominantly vertical/hierarchical; that is, human's place in the natural world is at the top of the hierarchy, and the natural world that exists around it is fundamentally subservient to the human race. Asian cultures with a heavy emphasis on Buddhist and Hindu philosophy would be characterized as horizontal/parallel cultures. This worldview places less of an emphasis on predominance of the human race over the world in which it exists. These differences can manifest their importance to business in a wide variety of ways, including the construction of effective promotional messages, the product features sought by different consumers, and the way in which the consumer buying process operates in the different cultures.

Aesthetics and Language

The last two ingredients of culture, aesthetics and language, are closely related. Unlike the other ingredients of culture, which are perhaps best characterized as involving values related to human interaction or behavior, aesthetics and language focus on values related to communication. Aesthetics refer to the values and meanings related to visual communication, whereas language provides a valuable insight into the values and meanings within a culture which can be gleaned from verbal communication. Of all the ingredients of culture, aesthetics is the most difficult to analyze.

It is hard to explain how best to understand and accommodate visual communications, but anybody who has spent even a short time in another culture understands the subtle, yet important, influence that aesthetics has in setting the proper environment to facilitate interaction. In other words, we—people—may not be able to describe our cultural aesthetics, but we know it when we see it. For example, earth-tone clothing is considered appropriate professional casual wear in the United States, but in many

European cultures, where business attire of all types is generally dark colors, it stands out. The best approach to really discovering the accepted aesthetic qualities in any given culture is observation of visual presentations of all types. This would include promotions and advertisements, clothing, signage, architecture—virtually anything set in the public domain with which it would have an element of communication or interaction associated. Being able to address the unique aesthetic characteristics of a culture can be of tremendous assistance in successfully operating within another culture.

The language aspect of culture and its importance in navigating that culture is too often viewed as a matter of proficiency. Understanding another culture, especially from a business standpoint, is generally not about language fluency. Although having the ability to speak a non-native language with a reasonable amount of fluency can be beneficial in any cross-cultural activities, this level of knowledge is not required for international business success. Rather than a focus on proficiency in reading and writing the language of a selected country of operation, it is more valuable to take into account the lessons about that culture that the language can provide. The role of language is as the verbal conveyor of cultural values and meanings. As such, simply understanding the basics of a language can provide great insight into how the culture interweaves the other four ingredients into its overall unique culture.

By learning the basics of any language, it is possible to gain insight into how that culture views and describes the world in general, how it "thinks" in areas related to the tangible and intangible as well as human interactions, the importance of individuals versus society and social groups—and this is just a very limited list. A phrase such as "Buy American" shows a great deal of how American consumers can, and have been, influenced toward certain firms and their products. The heavy use of "I" and "time" in English further reinforces the notion of the importance of self and structure in U.S. culture. Alternatively, the reluctance on the part of Japanese to use the word which would refer to "I" or "me" when speaking is a simple but powerful indication of a cultural hesitancy toward emphasizing self. Every culture has a unique worldview and having a basic—not necessarily fluent—knowledge of their language goes far from the perspective of an outsider trying to come to terms with this unique worldview.

Understanding the Key Areas of Cultural Differences in International Business

Now that we have a better idea of how to begin to understand cultural differences, in a way that goes beyond just a haphazard recognition that differences may exist, it is time to take the next step. This involves understanding how these cultural differences may affect business operations and how to deal with these differences. We look here at three fundamentally important areas of the international business environment and how culture has an impact on the firm's view of the competition, internal workforce management, and external consumer and market connections. Specifically, our focus turns to culture and competitive advantage, culture and organizational challenges, and culture and market/marketing activities.

Culture and Competitive Advantage

A good place to begin any attempt at deciphering the direct operational impact of cultural differences on a firm's efforts in the selected international market, or markets, is from the perspective of the competition either as a whole or a subset of individual firms. Taking this approach can have several advantages. First, assuming the competition is either indigenous, or has already entered the market, a wealth of knowledge related to how companies with similar product offerings approach that market and its consumers can be tremendously insightful. Clearly there is no need to "reinvent the wheel" if it is possible to observe existing market and marketing strategies with an eye to making improvements rather than starting from scratch. Similarly, by observing and analyzing how other businesses have approached that market, it is also possible to learn from their mistakes. Perhaps even more important than identifying the key factors for success in any international market is the need to avoid mistakes, which can be financially onerous but can also be difficult to overcome in anything more than a long time frame. Last, gaining a good understanding of the competition's activities in the market will also provide a basis for understanding how they will compete. Your competitors' action in the market tells a great deal about what they each consider their distinct strengths and weaknesses and gives an insight into how to create a unique strategy with the targeted consumers in that market. In order to have the best chance to fully understand your competition's actions within another cultural environment considering their competitive "mind-set" relative to cultural differences helps establish a picture of how those differences are incorporated into overall strategy.

There are three basic ways in which a firm can strategically approach a different cultural environment and deal with the challenges that could potentially arise. Similar to how a company might approach overall international operations (i.e., domestic extension, multidomestic, or global strategy) each provides insight into how the firm that takes a given approach sees cultural differences affecting their international business activities. The first is referred to as the "international" approach to cultural differences.

The firm that adopts this international approach treats cultural differences within the business environment with an "us versus them" mentality or, alternatively stated, a domestic versus "foreign" perspective. In this strategic mind-set, cultural differences are considered to be problematic—any deviation from known cultural beliefs, values, or influences has the potential to cause difficulties.

This generally leads firms that take this view to operate within a different culture by dealing with the cultural differences in a "management-by-exception" mode. In creating strategic plans for the market, the firm with an international approach will often create strategies that attempt to avoid cultural conflicts. This can result in compromises in the business model, particularly in the key areas of marketing—product, promotion, price, and distribution. These compromises, in turn, can easily result in poor, or incomplete, market penetration. Thus, when cultural differences result in problems within the market, the firm will only allocate resources to deal with the issue after the fact. This failure to deal proactively with differences in the cultural environment can create areas of opportunity for the firms who are prepared to accept, anticipate, and plan for the impact a different culture may have on company operations.

A second perspective on cultural differences is the multidomestic approach in which a firm will adopt market-specific strategies for dealing with differences in the cultural environment. Like an overall multidomestic business model, the multidomestic approach to the cultural environment assumes that the cultural differences in a given market require unique strategies and tactics to reach the consumers in that market. Even if it can be established that there are cultural differences that are relevant for the firm and its product offering in a market, it is important to recognize that applying this approach is resource-heavy and can tie the firm to that market. This combination generally means the firm is able to operate only in a limited number—perhaps only one—market(s).

The third, and last, approach to cultural differences is the global, or dynamic, approach. Here the determination is made that the corporate core, and fundamental product offering, can be "translated" across cultural differences. Although this can be an effective means of dealing with cultural differences if implemented properly, it can lead to opportunity costs (e.g., potential consumers can be "missed" because specific culturally oriented requirements are ignored) and under this approach, it can be more difficult to direct resources at individual "problem" markets that may demand a more tailored approach on the part of the firm.

How the competition chooses to deal with cultural differences in the international business environment can provide valuable insight into how that firm, or group of firms, intends to craft their strategy in that market. To fully contextualize cultural differences and their impact on competitive advantage, there are three basic lessons on which to build. First, culture and cultural differences should not automatically be assumed to be a relevant threat. There can be many cultural differences across markets that have no bearing whatsoever on a specific firm and its product offering. Next, viewing cultural differences from different perspectives (i.e., not only from the perspective of the firm itself but also from that of its competition) can result in a more effective understanding of how best to solve the problems that relevant cultural differences can present. Finally, different sets of values across cultures may mean greater opportunities, not greater risks. For example, a different gift-giving season between the United States and another culture can mean a positive offset in the retail sales cycle the U.S. market experiences leading up to the Christmas holiday.

So in navigating the global business environment—and in particular the challenges that the cultural environment may present—what can a firm do to create competitive advantage? The answer is to create a strategic mind-set that acknowledges, and to some extent embraces, these cultural differences and incorporates them into dealing with both internal/organizational and external/market activities in another market. This can be accomplished by leveraging the strengths of cultural differences and placing control or operations where local culture has unique strengths. For example, although the Chinese market is often viewed as a source of inexpensive labor, it is easy to overlook the loyalty and commitment that Chinese workers often show to their employer. Furthermore, it is possible to use cultural differences to reduce cycle time and improve problem solving (e.g., U.S. culture is decision/closure driven, which has the potential to delay decisions and response time). As we shall see later in the chapter, cultural differences can also be used to help develop more effective marketing and business strategies through the generation of new ideas (i.e., products such as McDonald's breakfast burrito) that can be used in other markets in which the firm operates. Having considered cultural differences in the larger context of the competition and competitive advantage, the discussion now turns to understanding cultural differences within the firm and in the larger market environment.

Culture and Organizational Challenges

Because a large part of any discussion of culture involves dealing with human interaction, navigating cultural differences across cultures, but within the same organization, can be particularly challenging. Other cultures may have characteristics that make individuals from that culture especially desirable as employees, or it may be that placing operations within that market naturally results in having a significant number of employees being drawn from the local workforce. In either case, firms that find themselves in the position of managing employee groups from separate and distinct cultures can quickly encounter conflicts between these cultures. This means that to manage effectively across cultures, the firm must be cognizant of the different types of internal conflicts that may be encountered. Generally, these typical conflict points within an organization fall into one of four categories: value conflicts/interpretations, conflicts related to the concept of structure, conflicts related to rewards, and conflicts related to the concept of valuable skills. First we consider the nature of these conflict points and then some ways in which a firm might deal with cross-cultural conflicts within the organization.

Value conflicts, or cultural conflicts related to the interpretation of values, have the potential to create serious management difficulties because they cut right to the heart of human interaction and communication. These most commonly involve a situation in which one culture places a great deal of importance on a value, or set of values, while the other culture does not. Many of these types of conflicts—differing religious beliefs, modes of dress, for example—are obvious from the outset, but others may not be so clear. Yet they can have a potentially profound impact on the organization and the internal management environment. These can, in turn, create ethical dilemmas within the organization. For example, so-called "traditional" cultures often have a hierarchical view of the relationship between genders—males typically being viewed as "superior." This type of scenario could easily lead to a workplace environment that would, in some cultures, be viewed as hostile toward women—perhaps even fall into the category of sexual harassment. Any values, beliefs, or customs that involve human interaction and communication must be taken into account from the perspective of the workplace environment and managing employees.

The remaining three conflict points—structure, reward, and valuable skills—are more organizationally concentrated but no less important to consider. Conflicts related to the concept of structure often manifest within an organization as authority and "report" differences. Over the years, one of the most powerful management tools in U.S. companies has been the development and refinement of the organizational chart. Most firms, from the small to the very large, use organizational charts to communicate to their employees exactly where their job/position fits into the overall business itself. This helps to clarify not only individual roles in the firm but also lines of authority. However, not all cultures are as structure oriented, which can lead to authority and management problems as well as negatively affecting decision making and response time.

Conflicts related to the concept of rewards frequently are highlighted across cultures in the value placed on intrinsic versus extrinsic rewards. Materially oriented cultures, such as the United States, motivate and reward employees extrinsically with "tangible" rewards (e.g., pay raises and bonuses). Not all cultures seek out this type of overt reward. In fact, in many more socially oriented cultures an extrinsic reward can be viewed negatively because it can be seen to separate the individual from his or her work, or social, group. When these conflicts based on the different cultures' concept of what is, or is not, an appropriate and sought-after reward surface, it can severely hamper the manager's, and the entire organization's, effectiveness in motivating employees through this change in culturally accepted management tools. Often, this is a difficult situation for managers to understand given that the source of the misunderstanding is at the heart of their own personal value system. Having a clear picture of how best to motivate and reward employees is fundamentally important for successfully managing individuals from other cultures.

The last of these "concept" conflict areas is in the area of valuable skills. In U.S. and many Western organizations, the most valued functional areas in a business are marketing and finance/accounting. Within the context of a material culture, this makes sense—it is easiest to place an actual monetary value on employees in these areas given their responsibilities for generating and managing sales and revenue. In this type of organizational culture, much less direct emphasis tends to be placed on other "soft" functional areas such as human resource management. In more socially oriented cultures, the emphasis is just the opposite. Here, the "fast track" to the top is more likely to be through human resources—the logic being that an organization is only as good as the employees it attracts, rewards, and retains. Either perspective is equally valid provided it is applied in the appropriate cultural setting. Placing too much emphasis on the "wrong" skill set can quickly alienate workers in that culture.

In any of these typical cultural conflict areas within an organization, the potential exists for disruption of the firm and its international business efforts. Navigating these differences begins with identifying the most likely conflict points. Successfully finding a way through these conflict points means proactively creating the appropriate organizational culture using either a value-, process-, or dependency-based approach. Understanding the issues related to operating within the international business environment means identifying potential problem areas and having a plan for dealing with these challenges.

The value-based approach for dealing with cultural differences within an organization essentially involves creating a strong corporate culture. Historically, IBM has adopted this focus and, even though the corporate business model has evolved from large-scale hardware products to wireless technology and consulting services, this means of folding people from a wide range of cultural backgrounds drawn from the company's worldwide business locations remains. In the value-based approach the organization's objective is to have all its employees adopt a defined set of values that are derived by the company itself.

That is not to suggest that individual employees are expected to reject their personal set of cultural values. Rather, in their role as company employees—and whenever they are in that role—they are expected to act according to the established company values, or corporate culture. In the case of IBM, the firm articulates the values and beliefs that reflect the corporate culture, and these are then reinforced throughout the organization various ways. Over the years, IBM has used the slogan "think"—a call for innovation and application—to draw employees together and the concept of being an "IBMer" has resonated throughout the company for decades even to the point of forming the basis for a recent advertising campaign. The logic behind this value-based approach is that individual employees will be able to put aside any potentially problematic cultural differences provided they are presented with a viable set of cultural beliefs limited to, and representative of, the organization.

Alternatively, depending on the type of organization, a process-based approach for dealing with cultural differences within the organization may be appropriate. Whereas the value-based approach is about building a corporate culture around the organization itself, the process-based approach involves building a corporate culture around what the firm does. This can be most effective within a company whose activities focus on a defined set of activities, such as a manufacturing firm. The notion behind a process-based organizational culture is to focus on building a common technical or professional culture.

Goodyear Tire & Rubber Company is the largest manufacturer of tires in the world, accounting for approximately 40 percent of tires manufactured globally. The firm has an established presence in every continent around the globe and has, for years, been faced with the challenge of bringing together employees from vastly different cultures. Rather than trying to reconcile these differences, in managing their diverse workforce, the firm focuses on the fundamental process of tire manufacturing and three basic activities—designing, manufacturing, and selling tires. Every employee in the firm, regardless of location or culture, is involved in at least one of these activities and by emphasizing the tire manufacturing process Goodyear is able to bring these individuals together and create an environment that focuses on employees being able not only to see where they fit into the organization but also to have a basis for mutual understanding—at least within the corporation. This is the basic logic behind a process-based approach.

The third approach to dealing with cultural differences within an organization, the dependency-based approach, is perhaps the fastest means of dealing with these differences, but it has the potential for serious drawbacks as well. A dependency-based approach involves effectively "forcing" the existing corporate culture and associated values on employees outside of the home market and managing/monitoring their actions and activities through strong centrally controlled financial and planning systems. Essentially, the dependency-based approach is a corporate culture of "our way or the highway." Although this may not be the most culturally sensitive means of dealing with cultural differences, it may be appropriate in a situation in which the firm is growing at a rapid rate in multiple markets. Depending on the methods through which "our way" is presented, it may not be as culturally insensitive as it might appear on the surface. However, it does in essence require individuals from other cultures to buy into a set of values without taking into account their own personal values and beliefs. This can easily lead to resentment over time, and the single biggest drawback to the dependency-based approach is that it does little to foster employee loyalty, which can easily mean that when times get tougher, cooperation from the nondomestic workforce may be difficult to come by.

There is a fourth approach to dealing with cultural differences at the organizational level—ignore them. In most cases, ignoring a potential problem is not the best idea for a successful, or an aspiring, business. However, in trying to get a handle on cultural differences, it may be the most effective for certain companies. In reality, this approach is not about actually ignoring these differences. Instead, it is about allowing those best suited within the organization to take on the challenge rather than dictating from the top. For example, a firm that operates internationally using a franchised-based business model may find that the most efficient means of managing across cultures would be for the focus at the corporate level to be on product and processes and allowing the local franchise owner—situated within the local culture—to develop their own means of managing employees in that culture. Under this approach, firm activities and responsibilities are placed in the hands of those best suited to deal with the unique elements of each. That is, at the corporate level the focus is on overall market, product, pricing, and distribution issues, leaving the local owners/managers to work through the operational/personnel issues associated with cultural differences.

Culture and Marketing Activities: The Impact of Cultural Differences on Strategy

Navigating through cultural differences in the external marketplace can be challenging but does not have to be viewed as an insurmountable task. The secret, like international business in general, is a systematic approach. The key elements of the external marketplace are the individuals who would comprise the customer base—already discussed earlier in this chapter—and the activities that businesses use to connect with those customers. These external market activities are better known as the four Ps of marketing: product, promotion, place (i.e., distribution), and price. Each of these has facets that can be affected by cultural differences. By carefully reviewing and analyzing these facets, it is possible to create a deeper understanding of where and how cultural differences might affect the firm's external market strategies.

A good place to start when conducting this analysis of the external market from the perspective of cultural differences is with the product offering. To be clear, the product is the bundle of all values that a customer obtains from the firm. It is much more than just a tangible good—it is everything associated with the good or service, direct or indirect, offered by the firm. This being the case, cultural differences could potentially have an impact on product strategy just about anywhere, but the most common areas of difficulty are the physical product itself, the product line, product presentation, and product packaging. A change to the actual physical product—in the form of feature changes—may be necessary, particularly if the customers in this other market use the product differently from home market customers. Similarly, if the product is in a form that makes it hard for the customers to identify with, physical product changes may be required. For example, any firm offering a product that involves tastes and preferences (e.g., food, clothing) could easily need to make changes to their physical product to have an attractive product offering in another culture.

Expanding out from the individual product, most firms have more than one product offering. These multiple product offerings, or product line(s), are developed to maximize market opportunities—but they are typically created for the specific needs of a single market. That is, they are highly targeted at specific consumer wants and needs. Thus, it is conceivable that consumers in another market may require the same level of differentiation, but this differentiation would be demonstrated through a change in the product line. This might mean expanding the line through the addition of a product specifically tailored for that market. An example of this would be Foster's Lager's expansion of its product line in the United States by offering Foster's Bitter or Special Ale to give the overall product line a more "British" feel. This is done regardless of the fact that Foster's is an Australian beer—it is viewed as being Brit-like by American consumers. On the other hand, a firm might reduce its product line to remove irrelevant products. Coca-Cola has a much-reduced product line in most markets outside of the United States. The fact is, there is no need for such a high level of differentiation (e.g., caffeine-free diet Cherry Coke) in most other markets around the globe.

A product presentation, or "delivery," change may be necessary to show your product in a more favorable light. One major U.S. donut franchise found that Japanese consumers identify a donut shop with European pastries. Instead of selling donuts by the dozen in cardboard boxes and serving large disposable cups of coffee, the firm had to "deliver" the donuts on china plates and serve the coffee in small, china espresso cups. Similarly, a product packaging change might be advisable to make the product relevant. In the United Kingdom, the standard serving of beer is an Imperial pint (18 ounces). To sell pint cans of Guinness in the United States, the size must be reduced to a standard pint size (16 ounces). By beginning an evaluation of the impact of cultural differences in the firm's ability to connect with customers in a different market, the best place to start is with the actual product offering those customers would be seeking out.

Where understanding how cultural differences may have an impact on product, and product strategy is all about deciphering how consumers in another market may view the firm's value offering, coming to grips with the potential impact of cultural differences on promotional strategy is about the communication process related to that value bundle (i.e., the product). Navigating through the complexities of cross-cultural communications is a huge challenge. However, for a firm operating in a different cultural environment, this daunting task can be somewhat lessened by remembering that it is only necessary to focus on communications specific to the product itself. To that end, there are four areas in which the communication process, represented by promotional strategy, may require changes.

First, it may be necessary to alter the positioning of the product—the fundamental core of any promotional message. Cultural differences can often mean that the positioning of a product in one culture may not be relevant or appropriate in another. For example, cosmetics may be positioned as "makeup" in one culture and as "skin care" in another. The former would place an emphasis on the individual, whereas for the latter, the crux of the message would be more directed toward being healthy—a subtle but potentially important cultural distinction. Second, the presentation of the message may also need to be altered, such as different personal interactions being used in advertisements. Traditional cultures often find the cross-gender interactions used in Western advertisements to be overly familiar and inappropriate. Third, there may be cultural issues in branding. A good brand name is the personification of a product, and both the meaning contained in a name and language-related issues could demand the brand name be changed. Fourth, and finally, any visuals used in the communication process, related to aesthetic cultural differences, may also need attention. Simple things such as the graphics and pictures frequently used in promotions as visuals can convey a wealth of information and must be consistent with cultural expectations.

The final two Ps of marketing—place (distribution) and pricing—involve closing the loop and putting the product into the hands of the customer. Cultural differences can have an impact on distribution first in its perceived role within a culture. In the United States, consumers tend to view distribution as a "cost-added" activity, as exemplified by the popularity of outlet malls and the expression "cut out the middleman." On the other hand, distribution can be viewed as a value-added activity, as demonstrated by product-focused retail outlets such as rice stores in many Asian markets. Given that the nature of distribution may change across cultures, so might other aspects such as the expected location for products—a good example being the popularity of vending machines for a wide range of products in the Japanese market. Price is most affected by cultural differences through the country-of-origin effect. This occurs when consumers make attributions regarding the quality of a product based on their perception of the country from which the product originates. As a negative country-of-origin effect increases, the firm will likely have to reduce product price or find some means to take the product's perceived home country out of the equation. Alternatively, a positive country-of-origin effect may enable the firm to charge a premium for their product—à la the ability of Foster's Lager to charge a premium in markets outside of Australia simply because those targeted markets have a positive perception of Australian beer.

In reviewing how best to deal with cultural differences in the external market, there are four basic keys for strategic success. First, as we have seen throughout this chapter, culture is not an insurmountable barrier—a little knowledge goes a long way, and it is not necessary to be an overall expert in the culture of the selected market. Second, culture is dynamic, not static. Even a hostile cultural environment can change over time, as demonstrated by the change in attitude of U.S. consumers toward

Japanese, and more recently Korean, automobiles. Third, it is important not to let individual, or firm, attitudes and beliefs inhibit decision making in another culture. The most successful firms are open in their thinking when it comes to operating in another culture (e.g., identifying different product uses, reasons to purchase a product). Fourth, be willing to learn from other firms' mistakes—even if those firms are in another industry. Mistakes related to cultural differences can be catastrophic and difficult to fix. The best firms carefully study the success, and failure, of other firms in a market before constructing and implementing strategy in that market.

Summary

When the question is asked, "What makes the international business environment unique?" the most common answer managers give is "cultural differences." Every country, and the market it contains, has its own distinct culture and subcultures. However, not all of these cultural differences represent a potential problem, or indeed are always relevant for any given firm. This chapter provided frameworks for identifying important cultural differences that must be managed, those that may be ignored, and for seeing cultural differences not as an automatic threat but as an area of potential opportunity—both within the organization and in the external marketplace.

CHAPTER THREE

Managing the Physical Environment: Market Selection and Market Entry

Introduction

Whereas culture, and cultural differences, may be the aspect(s) of the environment most commonly associated with international business, the physical environment may be the one most frequently ignored or otherwise overlooked. The physical environment has the potential to have a significant impact on international operations at the firm-level yet because it, more than any other piece of the international business environment, is viewed as "uncontrollable," and thus any discussion is often limited to how it can negatively affect a firm's ability to reach its objectives in another market. However, simply accepting at face value that the physical environment may, or may not, be a threat to operations is not sufficient for a firm striving to be successful in the global marketplace. The successful firm seeks both to understand how the various components of the international business environment might affect operations and, by extension, consider how best to deal with any possible threat(s). In this chapter, we approach this issue of understanding and dealing with the physical environment in a market by first discussing the different means through which the physical environment can collide with business activities and, then, how to manage this "collision" through the process of market assessment/selection and market entry strategies. Although it may not be possible to actually change the physical environment of a market, it is possible to actively control for the physical environment's impact on firm operations by managing the markets in which the firm operates.

The Physical Environment: Time, Distance, Setting

On the surface, it would be easy to say that the greatest area of opera-tional influence that the physical environment has on the firm would be logistics and logistical operations. It is certainly the case that the effect of the physical environment on logistics-oriented activities is, perhaps, the most obvious area of impact. Summarizing the operational impact of the physical environment can be boiled down to three aspects: time, distance, and setting. Time, and its effect on operations, can be viewed from several perspectives. There is the issue of time difference in decision making. By extending operational scope around the world, time differences can create a challenge for decision making—especially for firms with more highly centralized home country control. Even markets that are relatively close, such as the eastern United States and Europe, still have to deal with a six-hour time difference. Additionally, time can come into play in terms of response/cycle time. When markets are geographically separated com-munication slows down, resulting in a higher potential for breakdowns in the value chain (e.g., inventory stock-out) along with slower responses to market changes and competitive threats. Finally, time can adversely affect the firm's ability to reach its international objectives through the real pos-sibility of delays in the implementation of decisions.

The impact of distance is closely related to that of time. The relationship between time and distance influences response time across markets along with communication and decision making. At the same time, the increased geographic space between markets that distance represents adds another dimension beyond its interrelationship with time: risk. Increased distance increases response time, which represents risk, but there is the added dimension of product risk associated with increased distances between markets. As the distance a product must travel through the distribution channel goes up so does the risk that the product will be damaged—or dis-appear—before it reaches the final customer. Under these circumstances, distance is more than just an indirect cost—it becomes a tangible risk factor.

The third overall piece of the physical environment is setting. This refers to the actual physical environment itself and the potential differ-ences when compared with the firm's home market. Setting can affect the ability of an outside firm to move product into that market, to disperse product within that market or even how the product is used by consum-ers in that market. Combined with time and distance, the setting of any given market forms the basis for understanding the physical environment of that market, the elements that must be analyzed, how these physical market characteristics might influence various functional areas within the firm, and how to manage any anticipated threats through proactive market assessment, selection, and entry strategies.

The Physical Environment: Elements to Consider

Any assessment of the physical environment of a market begins by understanding the various elements that comprise this "physical" environment. Broadly speaking, these elements can be placed into three categories: geographic, human, and operational. Although each is part of the physical environment, their inclusion recognizes that this assessment must go beyond the basics of market terrain. To be effective, any attempt to fully understand and navigate through the physical environment of another market must take into account all facets that form this particular piece of the overall international business environment.

Geography or geographic influences on international business operations are, possibly, those most commonly associated with the physical environment. The main geographic influences would be location, topography, and climate. Understanding the physical environment starts first with understanding the nature of its location relative to other markets in which the firm either currently operates or intends to operate in the future. The location of a market plays a major role in determining its attractiveness both as an operational location as well as a source for revenue generation. The countries which adjoin any given individual market can impact a firm's ability to move resources and finished product in and out of that market. Location often also serves as an indicator of other countries with which that market may have established trading relationships—an insight into the competition the firm may face—and the political relationships that might exist between that and other markets. Within the market, the key geographic pieces are topography and climate. Clearly topography has the potential to influence distribution and logistical activities significantly, and climate can affect these concerns as well as influence a wide range of product strategy issues such as types of products, product features, and product sales cycle.

The human element of the physical environment comprises urban and human geography. Like location, understanding the challenges of the human aspect of a market starts with understanding the nuances of the population. Although it may be sufficient for an economist or a demographer to look at a country in terms of total population, a businessperson must take a more practical approach. Total population may be an early indicator of demand in a market, but it leaves out one of the most important issues for businesses—can those consumers be effectively reached? Understanding the human element of the physical environment may start with total population but must quickly move to issues related to population distribution and density.

Being able to identify "pockets" of consumers—or a population spread out over a large geographic area—enables a firm to manage the physical environment of markets through the market assessment and selection process. For example, China may be one of the most populated countries in the world, but many Chinese are not located in geographic areas that are easily accessible to outside companies. On the other hand, China does have extremely large pockets of consumers located within relatively easy reach on the eastern coast of the country. Thus, the "realizable" size of the Chinese market is not necessarily reflected in its total population. Similarly, Mexico, although no match for China in total population, does have a substantial concentrated market that rivals any other large concentrated market in the world—Mexico City, the fifth largest city in the world with a population of more than 17 million people. No Chinese city is in the top 10 for total population.

The other important piece of the human element relates to human geography or the characteristics of the individuals who comprise the country's population. Understanding a market's human geography helps to identify key trends that might influence both the composition of consumer segments as well as prospective employees. It also helps to create strategies for effectively connecting with consumers in the market. Overall demographic trends (e.g., aging), birth and death rates, education, literacy levels, family/living unit statistics, as well as other characteristics associated with describing an individual all feed into this idea of a full understanding of the people who comprise the human element of the physical environment and represent both potential consumers and potential employees.

The third element, operational, refers to those components of the physical environment that have the potential to influence directly the firm's operational efficiency. Although many facets of the international business environment can have an impact on firm operations, when considering just the physical aspect of the environment, two are featured most prominently: natural resources and infrastructure. For the firm engaged in manufacturing in this new market, the natural resources associated with that market can be key to efficient operations. If natural resources are important to the firm in assessing a given market, it is important to understand fully the issues related to natural resources. The question of availability of the required natural resources is obvious. What often gets lost, however, is the issue of accessibility of those natural resources. Canada is the home to what some estimate are the largest oil reserves in the world; the problem is that they cannot be accessed easily because the oil is located above the

Arctic Circle. Similarly, Russia has large deposits of a wide range of natural resources—oil, minerals, timber, and so forth. But like Canada, these are difficult to tap because they are located in Siberia. Simply possessing natural resources does not make a market attractive; availability means they both exist and are reasonably accessible.

Infrastructure involves the aspects of the physical environment that enable operational activities. A common oversight for firms from developed markets such as the United States and Europe is assuming the existence of necessary infrastructure. Although roads, bridges, power grids, and the like are aging in these markets, they have not yet deteriorated to the point that there is an absence that disrupts business. The absence of high-quality infrastructure—or any infrastructure at all—can be a difficult concept for many firms to understand. It is vitally important that this piece of the physical environment receive as much attention as the other components in any analysis of a market. This means reviewing any aspect of the physical environment that might affect the movement of product, people, or information. It would also mean analyzing infrastructure that might have an impact on both production capabilities and product usage capabilities.

How Does the Physical Environment Affect International Business?

Understanding the physical environment starts with tangible macrophysical elements such as market location, topography, and climate but—to be complete—it must also address the human and operational elements as well. To reinforce the significant influence that the physical environment may have on a firm, it may be useful to briefly consider its impact on several different functional areas of business. This clearly shows that the physical environment plays a crucial role in any firm's ability to operate successfully in a given market.

The accounting function can be affected by the physical environment when an aging population requires more social support, leading to increased taxes. Similarly, human resource management would also be affected when changing demographics require different employee benefit packages and the workforce in general changes. Finance, and financial management, can be affected by instability in the physical environment (e.g., Japan's propensity to suffer earthquakes) because this lack of stability can reduce the values of assets and investments which, in turn, would increase the cost of doing business in that market. The physical environment also has potentially substantial influence on marketing activities as it might affect product usage, product design, distribution strategies, and so on. There is really no area of business that cannot be negatively affected by the physical environment; it is the key to both economic development and market attractiveness. The only means through which a firm can control for the physical environment in its international operations is by carefully choosing the markets in which it intends to operate, making the market selection process and subsequent market entry strategy choice of paramount importance.

The Market Selection Process

One of the best ways of proactively managing the international business environment is through the market selection process. The logic behind this statement is simple: by choosing only markets that have a favorable business environment, the nondomestic firm is able to control the market threats it will be exposed to in its international operations. In this section of the chapter, we look at how firms should proceed in the market selection process and then consider the actual choice of a market(s). Before the discussion can proceed, however, there are some preliminary issues that must be taken into account. These relate to marketing, production, and strategy issues that will have an influence on which markets are considered, how these markets are evaluated, and finally which of these markets are selected by the firm requiring the creation of a market entry strategy.

These preliminary issues become important because they involve the basics that underpin the firm's international strategy and operational approach. In other words, placing the market selection process into the context of the firm's perspective on its international marketing, production, and overall strategy will guide the actual selection process and, later, market entry strategy. The dominating marketing issues, in terms of the market selection process, are focused on issues related to the market location, potential target market segments, and possible product synergies/similarities when the market in question is compared with other markets in which the firm already operates. Similarly, the production issues would deal with the potential for reducing time and distance risk through production operations—either total or partial—in the market under study along with the lowering of production costs and the value of "localizing" the production of the product. Both the marketing and production issues involve placing the previous discussion of the physical environment into a firm-specific context prior to engaging the market selection process.

This is also true of the strategy issues, although these are not as directly tied to actual operational activities; rather these would guide all operational activities including marketing and production. The strategy issues tied directly to the market selection process include the firm's international objectives for the market in question (i.e., operational location vs. revenue generator or a combination of both), the role of the international markets in the firm's overall operations (i.e., the amount of resources which can be expected to be devoted to the market), and other markets (both similarities and differences) in which the firm currently operates. The impact of, and relationship between, the physical market environment and firm operations was discussed earlier; it is at the beginning of the market selection process when these must be addressed at the firm level.

The Market Selection Process: Input Variables

The market selection process is built around four categories of input variables. These input variables cover the characteristics of the market, how these characteristics relate to firm operational activities, the capabilities of the firm itself relative to the market being assessed, and the various risk factors associated with that market. They comprehensively cover what needs to be assessed in an individual market to be selected by the firm as a target for international operations. At the conclusion of this step of the market selection process, the firm will have identified which, if any, markets are appropriate destinations. The second phase of the process, market choice, will involve picking which market, or markets, the firm will initiate operations in requiring the development of a market entry strategy.

The first of the input variables to evaluate deals with market size and sales potential. This assumes that revenue generation is at least part of the company's overall international objective; for most firms operating internationally, this is the case. Provided revenue generation is a priority, it makes good sense to begin the market selection process by assessing the market from the perspective of its attractiveness for income generation. This would involve a heavy concentration on the human geography of the market—population distribution and density, income size, distribution, disposable income, and expenditure patterns—as well as the level of market development, the source of economic activity (e.g., types of primary industries), and the sustainability of that economic activity. Many of the specifics of the economy and market attractiveness will be dealt with in more detail in the next chapter, but the ability of the market to support sustained income production is founded on the characteristics of the human geography—or groups of consumers—in the market.

The second input variable, external operational ease and compatibility, is all about how the characteristics of the market relate to the firm's operational activities. Again, the market's proximity and geographic characteristics—location, climate, topography, and so forth—must be compared with the firm's current markets of operation along with the firm's resources and expertise. There is also the issue of cultural and language similarities. Markets that have consumer segments with similar perspectives of the firm's product(s) represent the most attractive because the firm will be able to achieve a certain level of economies of scale by not having to make substantial product modifications. Furthermore, language similarities across markets also mean the ease of establishing and maintaining connections with the customer is greatly simplified. Last in this area are the market similarities (i.e., the operational part of the physical environment) that may allow the firm to standardize its activities across markets or, alternatively, require the firm to make changes in how it conducts business (e.g., product distribution, product features, promotional tactics).

The third input variable is directed not at understanding the market but in understanding the capabilities of the firm if it were to operate inside that market. Matching a market to an individual firm is much more than identifying a market with significant opportunity. Given the resources necessary to operate internationally, some markets may represent real opportunity yet be beyond the scope of the firm's available resources. It would be easy to focus the discussion of market selection solely on market characteristics, but the entire process must be oriented not just toward identifying "good" international markets. Rather, to be truly effective, this process should be conducted from the perspective of the firm.

With this in mind, determining the extent to with a market is compatible with a given firm's internal operations characteristics would address the following issues. First, the key characteristics of the market must be consistent with the company's capabilities. Note: we are looking at the *key* characteristics of the market. That is, those that could potentially hamper the firm's ability to succeed. This is not about identifying similarities and differences between the current market(s) of operation and the new market being evaluated. This is about taking into account fundamental characteristics of the market and determining the degree to which their impact might negatively affect the firm's chances for success.

For example, a leading real estate software firm in the United States was approached by a large institutional buyer based in Puerto Rico. The sale would have resulted in a significant increase in revenue of a five-year period, but the firm declined the order. Although the market size, sales potential, and other factors were all favorable, the company determined that the Puerto Rican market was not compatible with its internal operation capabilities—the firm had no Spanish-language expertise. Hiring the internal expertise was determined not to be viable, and outsourcing the necessary programming would have exposed the firm's proprietary source code. Thus, while the market held a great deal of potential, it was not a suitable fit for that particular company.

In this area of internal operation capabilities, there is also, naturally, the issue of cost and resource availability. The degree to which a market may, or may not, be relatively favorable for operations extend beyond just the issues discussed earlier related to external operational compatibility. The actual cost of doing business in that market must also be assessed, and that assessment must not be limited to financial costs. One important area that can be overlooked is not only the immediate direct costs associated with operating in another market but also the ongoing costs, such as opportunity costs incurred when resources are diverted away from an established market to fund operations in a new market. There is also the issue of required expertise, its availability, and the cost of obtaining or sourcing this expertise. The best international firms are able to identify and leverage their assets for maximum return, and a large part of this means selecting the market with the most opportunity for resource synergies.

This assessment of firm internal operational capabilities would not be complete without also considering the possibility of internal organizational obstacles and resistance. It is understood that no firm has unlimited resources. Any new opportunities being pursued by a firm will require the investment of a portion of these limited resources. Because of the nature of international business—it is resource heavy—and the fact that international operations often take substantially longer than domestic market initiatives to reap benefits, the plan to move into another market can quickly encounter organizational resistance. Resources will by necessity need to be diverted to the international initiatives, which may mean resistance from the areas within the business that are asked to make the sacrifice. It is also not uncommon for elements within the firm to attempt to block the movement into any given market simply because of an acquired prejudice toward that market—or international operations in general. Ascertaining the mood within the organization is crucially important for the effective long-term management of the market selection and entry strategy processes.

The last of the input variables in the market selection process are related to risk determination. Obviously, there must be more to market assessment than the overall characteristics of the market and matching these characteristics to firm capabilities. To a certain extent, this risk assessment can be viewed as a microcosm of the whole discussion of the international business environment. However, where our attempt to understand the various aspects of the international business environment is a holistic approach designed to prepare firms for successful long-term international operations, the risk assessment in the market selection process is focused on the operational risks attached to one particular market—when compared with other possible operational locations—from the perspective of one firm.

This risk assessment as part of the market selection process centers around a single market's competitive, monetary, and political risk. The assumption is that as the risk associated with each of these areas increases, the market becomes less attractive to the firm. The assessment of competitive risk should take into account the number and strength (e.g., market share) of the anticipated competitors as well as their priorities (e.g., the role of that particular market in their—the competitors—overall operations) and any source advantages they might enjoy. Monetary risk would be those factors that might make any revenue generated in that market vulnerable—liquidity restrictions, exchange rate stability, and the like. Political risk would be areas associated with the stability of the political system and the rules and regulations related to business—along with the propensity for enforcement—identified with the market. The overall goal of risk assessment in the market selection process is twofold: to obtain a clear view of what types of risks are most closely associated with a given market, and to have a basis for comparing market risks across multiple markets that may be part of the firm's market assessment and selection process.

The Market Selection Process: Choice

It is appropriate at this juncture to point out that the market assessment and selection process does not necessarily focus solely on one market. It is quite possible that, following an assessment of several possible markets, the firm may decide to enter multiple markets, or it may focus its efforts on just one. This strategic choice is the choice between a diversification and a concentration approach to market selection. Diversification would be when the firm opts for a relatively large number of markets with anticipated slow growth in each. A major U.S. video rental firm chose this approach as it allowed market risk to be spread across all its international markets. Concentration, on the other hand, involves selecting and entering just a few, perhaps only one, with anticipated fast growth in each. Initially, Foster's Lager adopted this approach in the United States, and later Great Britain, because these markets were determined to be the most receptive to the firm's premium positioning of its product as "Australian for beer."

A number of market factors should be considered when a firm considers a diversified versus a concentrated approach to market selection. The first of these relate to the characteristics of the market—specifically growth rate and anticipated sales stability. In many ways, these two factors go hand in hand. A steady, sustainable growth rate should help foster sales stability provided there is ample demand for the firm's product. One, or a limited number, of markets with these characteristics are often bundled together as high-priority markets in a market selection concentration strategy. It is rare for any firm to identify a large number of markets with such high levels of opportunity, so that when a limited number are identified, it makes sense to concentrate on these as an operational priority.

There is also the need to place the firm and its products into the context of each market under consideration. When the issue involves selecting the number of international markets to enter, the relevant factors can be reduced to two: competitive advantage and market synergies. The best markets are clearly those where the firm can quickly enjoy significant competitive advantage. High levels of universal brand equity (e.g., Starbuck's coffee in the early years of this century) can result in the best parts of both a diversification and a concentration selection strategy—lots of markets with fast growth. Unfortunately, this is generally not sustainable over time—or tempts the firm into aggressive growth, which saturates the market(s). Instead, competitive advantage should focus around aspects of the firm such as internal capabilities (e.g., Apple) and/or product "values" (e.g., Walmart). The scope, or the number of, markets in which a firm operates should only be increased as these internal capabilities or product values can be shown to be both relevant and sustainable.

Closely related to this notion of competitive advantage is that of market and product synergies. The best markets are those where the firm's core competencies can be leveraged to create synergies that might not exist in its home market. Honda is the classic example of such synergies. The firm's core competency has always been its ability to design and manufacture scalable internal combustion engines. Although that meant the manufacture of motorcycles, and then cars—initially small cars—in Japan, this knowledge has created synergistic opportunities in other markets like the United States, as well as other markets. This ability to scale engines up and down in size puts the firm in the position to create a wide-range of products—gas generators, lawn mowers, outboard motors, and so on— which may have limited appeal in Japan but can be sold in large quantities in these other markets. Any market where these synergistic effects can be realized should move to the top of the list in the market selection process.

There is also the nature of the market itself to consider in the market selection process. The best markets would be those where primary demand for the firm's product type is relatively high, enabling the firm to concentrate on marketing its own specific brand rather than expending resources directed at raising product awareness. This demand should also be established and sustainable—at least in those markets being given the highest priority. Other aspects related to the market's "climate" become relevant as well. This would not be a discussion solely related to the physical environment but would extend to aspects such as the nature of the competitive environment and consumer attitudes (e.g., the existence of a country-of-origin effect).

The choice of which market, or markets, to enter is generally not easy or obvious. Careful consideration must be given to not only the factors discussed here but also to the firm's overall business model, the role of international markets in that model, and how the market(s) being evaluated fit into that model. With this in mind, it is worthwhile to note the common errors firms make in the market selection process. Obviously, given the complexity of the process, any one of a number of mistakes could potentially occur. However, in the actual selection process itself, firms tend to err on two ends of a continuum. One side of this is when the firm will overlook markets that represent significant opportunity. This is often the result of the decision makers in the organization exercising their own personal cultural preferences or succumbing to prevailing stereotypes regarding a market (e.g., consumers in the market are too "poor" to be able to afford a particular product). On the other end are errors related to examining, and perhaps selecting, too many markets as "good" locations. This is typically the result of the firm in question having unfocused goals and objectives for its international operations and gathering too much data with no clear idea as to why the data is relevant.

The key to success in the market selection process is twofold: 1) have a clear understanding of what the firm seeks to accomplish in the international marketplace and 2) in evaluating markets, employ criteria that relate directly to the ability to accomplish these goals and objectives. Once this market selection process has been successfully completed, the next step is to develop a market entry strategy, which means understanding not just what might cause a firm to choose one form over the other but also the underlying differences between the market entry choices.

Understanding Market Entry Strategies

The discussion of market entry strategy is about understanding the different options available to a firm for placing itself into a nondomestic market. Although this means logistical issues and the physical movement of product play a large role in the discussion, market entry strategy is much more than setting up an international distribution channel. The market entry strategy developed by a firm involves how the firm "presents" itself to the consumers, competitors, suppliers, and others in an international market; that is, will the firm and its products adopt a "foreign" position, will it attempt to establish itself in a more integrated fashion, or will the firm assimilate itself and its product as much as possible in that market? This escalation of market involvement, which requires balancing increased risk and exposure with increased opportunities, is referred to as the *internationalization model*.

This internationalization model argues that as a firm's knowledge of international operations increases, so does its propensity to become more involved in (i.e., extend more assets into) their international markets. This knowledge is both objective (e.g., secondary) and experiential (e.g., primary). As these knowledge levels increase—particularly experiential knowledge—a firm will move toward higher levels of internationalization—that is, through exporting to some form of partnership and eventually foreign direct investment. As we will see, some firms, for many good reasons, never move beyond the initial step of exporting but the likelihood that any firm will move from domestic operations directly into foreign direct investment is remote. Using this internationalization model as a backdrop, our discussion of market entry strategy will be built around this notion of level of market involvement.

Market entry strategies revolve around three basic entry choices. These are exporting, strategic alliances or partnerships (vertical and horizontal), and foreign direct investment (i.e., assimilation). Perhaps the easiest way to conceptualize, or define, exporting is "build it here, sell it there." We will see that exporting is far more complex, but this simple definition communicates the fundamental goal of exporting—to maintain control by keeping as many assets and as much operational activities as possible within the firm's home market. Strategic alliances or partnerships, on the other hand, involve extending assets and operational activities into the host market through some type of collaboration with a local firm. The differences between vertical and horizontal partnerships lie in the way power and authority flow within the partnership. Finally, foreign direct investment is an entry strategy in which the firm attempts, as much as possible, to become local; that is, foreign direct investment (FDI) is about trying to take the "international" out of international business.

However, before we can begin to understand the nuances of each market entry strategy option, it is worthwhile to consider what influences firms to select one particular form of entry strategy over another. These are referred to as the determinants of market strategy, or market entry mode. They can be placed into one of two categories. The first, strategy variables, are firm-specific. This means these market entry determinants can only be addressed at the individual firm level and have the potential to differ from one firm to the next even if the two firms are in the same industry and/ or from the same home market. The second, environment variables, are market-related. The market-related variables can have similarities, especially across firms from the same industry or home market.

Firm-Specific Variables

Looking in more detail at each category shows that the firm-specific strategy variables take into account issues related to the firm's competition and competitive advantage as well as the firm's strategic goals for its international operations. The firm's competition, or competitive set, influences market entry strategy when the concept of global concentration of competition becomes part of the decision-making process. This notion of global concentration recognizes that no competitor, no matter how large, has unlimited resources. This means that, like any firm, the competition must prioritize where resources are allocated—some markets getting more attention, thereby being tougher to compete in, than others. In markets where there is less concentration of competition, a firm will be in a better position to commit to a given market faster, and at a higher level, than in a market where a high level of competitive concentration represents significant risk.

The nature of the firm's competitive advantage also has a significant impact on a firm's choice of entry mode. This perspective on competitive advantage is referred to as *global synergy*. As a firm begins to consider expansion into international markets, one of the first areas to be addressed is that of product concept. Determining the fundamental nature of the firm's distinct competitive advantage can reveal numerous product applications that may not represent actionable demand in the firm's home market but can be applied numerous ways in other markets. For example, Honda's core product competency—its distinct competitive advantage—is the design and manufacture of small internal combustion engines. In Japan this has meant the company's primary products over the years have been motorcycles and small cars. However, as the company expanded into the U.S. market, it saw lucrative applications of this core competency in a wide range of products (e.g., lawn mowers, outboards motors, generators). This increased number of applications represents product synergies for Honda, causing the firm to relatively quickly adopt a foreign direct investment entry strategy in the United States to be as close as possible to the unique opportunities that market represented compared with the home market of Japan.

Lastly, in the category of firm-related strategy variables, there is the issue of strategic goals. Clearly what a firm expects to get out of its international operations will heavily influence what it puts into those markets. Objectives centered around expanding sales, defraying inventory costs, or other goals would be most associated with an entry strategy such as exporting, which requires lower levels of commitment in terms of both time and other resources (i.e., capital). On the other hand, a firm that seeks nondomestic markets as an alternative to its domestic market would be more likely to commit higher levels of resources and assets to a market sooner and move through the internationalization model into some form of partnership or even foreign direct investment at some point.

Market-Related Variables

Moving to the next category of entry mode determinants brings us to the market-related or environment variables. As mentioned earlier, these environmental characteristics tend to be more generalizable across firms and industries originating from the same home market. As is the case for many decisions in international business, country risk is a factor in the choice of a market entry strategy. However, the two most important areas of country risk that have a direct impact on this choice would be economic and political risk. Economic risk, related to the stability, sustainability, and quality of demand, would cause a firm to seek a more controlled, risk-averse, entry strategy, such as exporting or a partnership that would help to diffuse any potential economic risk. Similarly, political risk related to restrictive or vague rules and regulations governing business activities might also lead a firm to stick to the lower levels of market immersion as outlined by the internationalization model.

Another important market-related factor would be location familiarity. As the internationalization model points out, higher levels of experiential knowledge of a given market would cause a firm to consider higher levels of operational immersion—including an assimilation strategy built around some form of FDI. In addition, knowledge of similar, or comparable, markets might serve as a basis for the firm to engage in a higher-level entry strategy. For example, firms with operational knowledge in one Middle Eastern market often find that much of this knowledge is applicable in neighboring countries. Finally, there are market trends related to demand uncertainty and competitive intensity that must also be taken into account. Developing an understanding of your firm and the proposed market through the analysis of these firm-specific and market-related variables helps to provide a solid foundation for selecting the market entry strategy best suited for the needs of any individual firm.

Exporting—A Home Market Focus

Having said earlier that exporting can be characterized as "build it here, sell it there," any further discussion must recognize the complexities involved in the exporting process. It is true that exporting represents the lowest level of involvement from the perspective of market entry strategy. It can be effective in controlling for the many risks associated with the international business environment and can be the most cost-effective means of extending firm operations beyond the domestic market. To understand these complexities better, the best place to begin is with an understanding of the various tasks that must be performed for any exporting program to be successful. These tasks involve all facets of operations from moving the product through the supply chain and into the hands of the customer and fall into three categories—logistical, transactional, and support.

Exporting Tasks

The most prominent export task involves logistics and is the foundation for the notion of "build it here, sell it there"—that is, product shipment. This involves physically moving the product from the point of manufacture to the selected market. Product shipment-related tasks would include the logistics of transporting the product internally within the domestic market to the point of embarkation, transportation between the home and host market, and disembarking the product in the host market. To accomplish this first logistical task successfully, there are the issues of the actual transportation to coordinate along with managing product damage and shipment shrinkage at the accompanying issues of product ownership and insurance, for example.

Just the logistics of physically moving the product from the market of manufacture to the market in which it will be sold can be a significant challenge, but the logistical tasks associated with exporting are not yet finished. There is still the question of local distribution. Simply placing the product in the host market is not enough. The product must then be distributed throughout the market. This requires not only physically moving the product out into the host market, it means establishing the necessary distribution channel in which the product can consistently flow through the various wholesalers and retailers to the final customers. The difficulties identified with the distribution aspect of exporting can be overlooked, but the crucial importance, and relational nature of, distribution—with the wholesalers and others who will move the product and the retailers who will sell it—means that the truly successful exporting firm quickly recognizes that exporting is not just an exercise in physically moving the product between markets.

Within, and at the end, of this distribution process is the second category of exporting tasks that must be performed—transactional. The fact that exporting often involves working through local firms within the distribution channel—sometimes removed multiple times from direct interaction with your firm—which means that completing the sales of your product and cycling the resulting revenue back through that channel, ultimately to your firm, is a task that it is essential not to overlook. Being separated from the market and the multiple transactions that must take place for your product to be placed in the hands of the consumer is a serious challenge for any firm that selects exporting as its market entry mode. It is important that the entire transactional process, from when the product leaves your firm's control until the final end user acquires the product, be mapped out and accounted for in terms of costs and revenue flow.

The third set of export tasks is support-related. Getting a product into the hands of your targeted consumers—successfully and over time—begins with logistics and payment. However, the sustainability of the process is in large part dependent on these support tasks. They start with the administrative and legal tasks involving actual product movement (e.g., insurance) and extend to areas such as customs and other tasks related to product entering the market in question as well as executing and monitoring contractual arrangements between your firm and members of the supply chain. Other administrative tasks that must not be forgotten include the development and execution of promotional strategies for your product and after-sale support. Having a good understanding of the tasks required for any export program is absolutely necessary for any firm before considering exporting as a potential market entry strategy. Not only does this increase the likelihood that an exporting program will be more successful, analyzing each of these tasks in the context of the host market from the perspective of your specific firm creates a much better understanding of the business environment of that individual international market.

Approaches to Exporting

We have assumed that the choice to export—and the approach to exporting adopted by the firm—is a conscious and deliberate decision on the part of the firm to be actively involved in the sale of its product in another market. However, this is not always the case. Under certain circumstances, a firm may find its products are being "passively" exported to another market. One means through which this takes place is in filling orders from domestic buyers. The firm may receive attractively sized orders for product from a buyer in its home market, who then sells the product in another market—sometimes without the producing firm being aware its products have gone international. These sales are often indistinguishable from domestic sales and can represent not only lost opportunities in the markets in which the products are being sold but also a loss of control over product pricing, positioning, and other concerns if the firm decides in the future to enter that market. Having control over all aspects of your product is an essential first step in any export program.

An active export program can be built around one of two approaches to exporting—indirect or direct. Indirect exporting involves engaging an intermediary to perform a wide-range of functions that may include market and/or customer identification, market research, and distribution. These intermediaries generally are agents, export management companies (EMCs), or export trading companies (ETCs). In the case of any of these intermediaries, the advantage is that they provide local knowledge and local relationships, thereby lowering potential risk in the market—but at the expense of a certain level of control. Furthermore, each has its own unique characteristics that must be taken into account.

Agents generally represent one or more firms in a given market and are paid commission most commonly on the value of sales. Using an agent is relatively easy, which is why doing so is a common form of indirect exporting. However, there are some caveats in dealing with these agents. One is the difficulties that can be encountered in terminating the relationship. The other is the fact that many agents represent several firms, which can lead to a conflict of interests in giving your product full support in the market. An EMC exports products on behalf of your firm through a contractual arrangement, which can mirror that of an agent (i.e., paid on a commission basis) or as a distributor (i.e., taking title to the product and earning revenue through resale). EMCs can also provide a range of other consultative services and frequently specialize in particular industries or in particular product types. Engaging an EMC means basically outsourcing all aspects of your firm's market entry strategy—which can be a huge advantage but can also mean your firm becomes overly dependent on the EMC and fails to develop any type of international operational expertise. At the highest level is the ETC. EMCs are generally restricted to performing export-related activities, but ETCs provide a full range of services, including importing, exporting, assistance with countertrade, the creation and implementation of supply chain strategy, and financing. These can be formidable partners and are common particularly in Asian markets.

Direct exporting, on the other hand, is an approach in which the firm assumes internal control over the entire exporting process. It is important to note that this does not necessarily mean the firm sells directly to the final customer. Direct exporting means that the firm assumes full responsibility—either itself or through a distribution channel similar to a domestic market—for getting its product to local buyers rather than using the services of an agent, EMC, or an ETC. Any firm involved in direct exporting will testify to the fact that exporting is not as quick and easy as it might appear on the surface—it is a long-term, committed strategy with higher levels of control than the indirect approach but also demands more resources and has higher levels of risk attached.

Executing a direct export plan requires the firm to establish a mechanism through which product and revenue can move. The tools firms most commonly employ to perform the required tasks in direct exporting are sales representatives and/or distributors. Sales representatives differ from agents in that they will represent your product exclusively. When using a sales representative the firm retains title to the product and compensates the representative through some combination of salary and sales commission. Using this arrangement means the firm maintains a much higher level of control over the way its products are marketed but also adds what amounts to an additional layer of employee(s) in the host market. Distributors do take title to the product and then sell the product at a markup, which represents their revenue. Their incentive to market the product in a way that is consistent with the goals of the manufacturing firm comes in the fact that both current and future sales—and consequently revenue— are dependent on the manufacturing firm providing product.

Indirect versus Direct Exporting: Factors to Consider

The process of choosing between indirect and direct exporting is influenced by several factors. First, there is the issue of the size of the firm—or more accurately the export-related resources available to the firm. Firms with a relatively high level of financial resources will be more able to commit to a market using a direct exporting program, which is more expensive than indirect exporting. However, important export-related resources go beyond just finances. There is also both objective and experiential knowledge to consider. A firm may not have high levels of financial resources, but high levels of knowledge may enable it to enjoy the advantages of direct exporting. A second influencing factor is related to the nature of the firm's product. Products which require higher levels of attention, or control, as they move through the distribution channel are better suited to direct exporting. Third, there are the business conditions of the market to take into account. Instability in any given market would cause a firm to be less reluctant to commit assets to that market and make indirect exporting a more logical choice for its market entry strategy. Both indirect and direct exporting are reasonable means for building your firm's international market entry strategy. The trick is to select the one that best fits your firm and its resource base, the needs of your product, and the nature of the international business environment in which you have chosen to operate. There is also the need to avoid the common mistakes associated with exporting.

Common Mistakes in Exporting

Considering that exporting is traditionally seen as the best means for firms new to international operations to enter a host market, it is natural that mistakes are made. Some of these can be attributed to a lack of knowledge and experience, others due to a failure to take into account the commitment necessary to be successful in another market, and still others are the result of the firm taking too narrow a view of its capabilities when it comes to international operations. Here are the most common mistakes made by firms that export.

- Failure to develop an international marketing plan
- Insufficient commitment by top management
- Insufficient care in selecting an overseas distributor(s)
- "Chasing" orders
- Neglecting export business when the domestic market "booms"
- Failure to treat international partners/distributors on an equal basis with domestic partners/distributors
- Assuming what works well in one nondomestic market will work well in all nondomestic markets
- Being unwilling to modify products to meet local regulations and/or cultural preferences
- Failure to print service, sale, and warranty messages in a locally understood language
- Failure to consider an export management firm
- Failure to provide readily available service for products
- Failure to consider a strategic alliance

A lack of knowledge or experience is an understandable cause for problems in any business endeavor, but any failure to perform straightforward preparations before entering a new market is difficult to defend. With that in mind, it is vital for any firm to undertake the necessary planning and "due diligence" before engaging in an export program. As we have seen, exporting may be the least involved market entry mode, but it is hardly simple. Additionally, it may be tempting to opt for the "sure thing" that the home market represents, but neglecting an export market—or worse, "chasing" orders in various markets—demonstrates little commitment to international markets, and it can be expected that intermediaries in that market will reciprocate. Last, a firm may hit on a successful product and marketing formula in one market but is naive to think that the international business environment does not vary from market-to-market and, therefore, requires adaptation of the marketing mix across markets.

Strategic Alliances—Vertical versus Horizontal Partnerships

The next step beyond exporting, in terms of involvement in an international market(s), is a strategic alliance. These can be in the form of either a vertical or horizontal partnership, but at their core, all strategic alliances are the same and require the same components to be effective. For our purposes, a strategic alliance can be best defined as a long-term explicit arrangement among distinct for-profit organizations that allows each to gain advantage over other firms outside the alliance. The key to understanding the importance of this definition is threefold. First, the strategic alliance enhances long-run competitiveness; second, each party provides unique contributions (e.g., technology, expertise, market access, capital) to ensure competitive advantage; and third, there is some level of mutual decision making. These are obtained within a strategic alliance when the partner firms focus on building the partnership around specific core dimensions.

The Core Dimensions of a Strategic Alliance

The best strategic alliances are built first and foremost around the goal compatibility of the partners. On the surface, this sounds overly simplistic—that each partner needs to have the same goal for the partnership to be functional. In this case, the problem does not generally lie directly with goal compatibility; rather it lies in how progress toward the goal is measured. For example, two partner firms seek to maximize revenue over time. However, one firm measures this success in terms of high levels of sales revenues and the other in terms of high levels of product sales or customers. Increasing sales revenues is typically approached using a skimming price (i.e., a relatively high price that is lowered over time) while increasing number of products sold—or customers—is achieved through penetration pricing (i.e., a relatively low price that is raised over time). Either represents a means of measuring success, but they are inherently incompatible.

Assuming goal compatibility—and the means to measure goal achievement—can be agreed on, the next core dimension would be strategic advantage. Ideally, a strategic alliance will provide competitive synergies for the partner firms that create strategic advantage. To gain this strategic advantage, firms seek partners with complementary competitive competencies. For example, several years ago Ford Motor Company formed an alliance with Mazda. From Mazda's perspective, Ford brought financing and a major global dealer network to the table; Ford, in turn, sought Mazda's design expertise. Both firms saw synergies in overall product line— Ford with trucks and mid- to full-size sedans and Mazda with cars that tended to be smaller and sportier. The end result was benefits to both firms that could be leveraged in a number of markets around the globe.

This notion of strategic advantage is tied to the third core dimension— interdependence. The most functional strategic alliances are difficult for either partner to terminate. When significant strategic advantage is gained through the partnerships this interdependence naturally follows, and although it signals a potential loss of direct control on the part of the individual firm, the fact that this interdependence exists is a sign that the partnership has created advantages that are beyond the scope of either firm when operating as a single entity.

The last two core dimensions that should be built into any strategic alliance are commitment and coordination. A partnership, of any kind, does not really exist unless there is a willingness on the part of each partner to invest in that partnership. This is also true in the case of strategic alliances. However, it is important to recognize that because each partner seeks complementary resources that can be leveraged for strategic advantage, any investment by either partner will necessarily take different forms—and therefore must be measured in terms of benefit to the partnership and not strictly in financial terms. Instead, commitment is better measured from the perspective of critical resources. That is, has each partner invested resources into the alliance that are critical to their individual firm? Firms that make capital investment in a strategic alliance can clearly demonstrate their level of commitment. At the same time, any firm that provides access to its distribution channel has also invested heavily in the partnership, but this investment may be more difficult to measure in a strictly financial sense. The key to commitment in strategic alliances is this idea of investing critical resources.

The concept of coordination—the last core dimension of strategic alliances—is about the ongoing functionality of the partnership. There are three areas in which coordination must exist in order for the alliance to be effective and efficient over time. It starts with the coordination of planning. Both sides must be actively involved in developing the long-term vision of the partnership—goals and objectives as well as the benchmarks and milestones to be used for measuring progress toward these goals. There must also be coordination of implementation—that is, not only agreement as to how to meet the established goals but also mutually coordinated activities on the part of both partner firms targeted at meeting these goals. Finally, the best strategic alliances have an established protocol for conflict resolution. Over time, it is natural for conflicts to arise between partner organizations. Coordinating how to address these conflicts before they arise means that they are more likely to be dealt with in a timely fashion without disrupting the activities of the alliance and, perhaps more important, prevent the partnership from dissolving because of what could easily be just an isolated incident of conflict.

Each of these core dimensions of a strategic alliance has a distinct purpose. Whether it is understanding the benefits to be derived by the partnership, recognizing the need to ensure mutual benefits for participating firms, creating an arrangement that will be more likely to exist over time, or including the necessary structure for the alliance to function effectively are each critical foundational pieces. How these are balanced based on the specific partners—and what each partner has to offer—becomes a question of which type of strategic alliance is most appropriate given the market conditions and the distinct competencies associated with those partner firms.

Common Types of Strategic Alliances

Strategic alliances can come in several types, but they all fall into one of two categories. Vertical alliances, such as licensing agreements, are those in which one partner has more "power" within the partnership. That is, the fundamental basis for the alliance is initially controlled by that particular firm. For example, in a licensing agreement the initial basis for the existence of the partnership is whatever is being licensed. Thus, the vertical alliance is so called because one partner is "higher" than the other. That being said, it is important to understand that although this hierarchical arrangement exists, it will not be functional over time if the dominant partner exerts too much authority. A horizontal alliance (e.g., a joint venture) is one with a more balanced interaction between the partners from the outset. Because they involve less resource commitment over time, and because they are more likely to be the next step when firms move away from exporting to become more involved in their international market(s), vertical alliances are a good starting point for understanding this type of market entry mode.

The most common types of vertical alliances are licensing, franchising, and contract manufacturing. Licensing is a contractual agreement in which the host-market firm receives the right to use some piece of their partner firm's property (e.g., technology, brand name, product or facility design). The property may be tangible or intangible. A licensing agreement is most appropriate in situations in which one particular aspect of the home market firm's operations gives it distinct competitive advantage, such as the brand equity attached to Levi's brand name. Franchising, on the other hand, is the total licensing of a complete business model—one that is proven in the home market. Often times, the firms that successfully franchise have a large service, or intangible, component associated with their product. Subway has been one of the leading franchises worldwide for years. Subway's business model combines the concept of fresh ingredients and health with a product that is prepared to order. This combination of healthy ingredients and freshness (i.e., service preparation), along with a recognized brand name, create a unique turnkey business model that is relevant across multiple markets. Contract manufacturing, as the name implies, is associated with firm that mass produces a tangible good. In this type of strategic alliance, the firm contracts with a host firm to produce its product. This has a number of advantages. Contract manufacturing requires minimal investment on the part of the firm contracting out its production and, at the same time, allows for brand-name control and helps to control for any possible negative country-of-origin effect. Contract manufacturing also helps to avoid currency risks that, in turn, can reduce cross-market pricing issues.

The most common horizontal strategic alliance is a joint venture. These involve shared ownership and control. It is not uncommon in developing markets for the government to require some type of joint venture to control the market activities of nondomestic firms and the flow of currency across its borders. Successful joint ventures are built around technical partnerships, which require contributions from both partners, and emotional partnerships, which require mutual commitment. This is a long-term, highly committed type of market entry strategy that is the most involved sort of foreign direct investment.

Advantages of Strategic Alliances

So why would a firm engage in a strategic alliance as its market entry strategy? There are numerous advantages to forming some type of strategic alliance. First, there is the opportunity to share large capital investments. Pooling the financial resources of two firms in the same market provides the potential for having a larger presence in the market faster, even if both firms don't have equal access to capital. There is also the advantage associated with access to complementary resources. As discussed earlier, the truly functional strategic alliances provide unique competitive advantages to both partners—whether financial, product, distribution, or market related. These strategic alliances enable firms both to reduce and to spread risks. Reduce risks through the relationships and market knowledge your local partner possesses and divide risks between both firms. Finally, strategic alliances enable your firm in many cases to co-opt the competition because your local competitors are the most natural fit for a partner, resulting in a win-win situation. The strategic alliance is the next step beyond exporting in our discussion of market entry strategies. However, there is one step left that may be an option for your firm—FDI. This market entry mode is associated with the highest levels of control and potential but carries with it the highest levels of commitment and risk.

Foreign Direct Investment—Assimilation

The most involved approach to market entry, one designed to remove the "international" from international business, is FDI. The overall goal of foreign direct investment is assimilation. That is, to become as local as possible within the host market. There are tremendous advantages to this approach. FDI enables the firm to become much closer to its customer base, to develop closer ties within its supply chain and distribution channel, to avoid many of the trade barriers attached to imported products, and to reduce any potential negative country-of-origin effect—and this is just a partial list. However, FDI also requires substantial investment, financial and otherwise, on the part of the firm and once implemented it is difficult to step away from a market in which direct investments have been made. It may be relatively easy for an exporting firm to stop the flow of product to a given market, but a firm with an FDI-based entry strategy has a hard time simply ceasing production without incurring large costs immediately and over time. FDI can take the form of a "build" (i.e., the purchase or creation of physical assets such as a manufacturing facility à la BMW's presence in the Carolinas) or a "buy" (acquiring ownership share in a local business à la Walmart's purchase of ASDA in Great Britain). Regardless of the build versus buy decision, both approaches demand high levels of resource commitment and the question then becomes why would a firm take this type of risk.

Why FDI?

A firm might choose to risk the level of resources demanded by an FDI entry strategy for several reasons. One is related to the international product life cycle. In a firm's home market, particularly if it is a developed market, it is more likely for it product(s) to be in the mature stage of the product life cycle. This means for product sales to continue, or grow, the firm must find new uses for the product, new target market segments for the product, or new markets entirely. This third option causes many firms to move outside of their domestic market and can naturally lead them to FDI given the potentially unique requirements of a host market and the importance being placed on that market for future sales. Another good reason for engaging in FDI is the desire for internalization. By placing operations (i.e., "internalizing" operations) within the host market, the firm is able to remove the problems of trade barriers and other market imperfections that exist when market boundaries are crossed. There is also the possibility that through FDI, the firm will experience some location advantages from placing operations within the host market. These might take the form of location advantages associated with the market's characteristics (e.g., availability of raw materials, unique aspects of local consumers), the ability to acquire competitive advantage (e.g., local labor skills), or through some form of ownership advantage (e.g., brand equity). Finally, the ability to gain market power using an FDI approach through forward integration, backward integration, or both should not be ignored. Given these potential advantages—and the risk already discussed—what would cause a firm to conclude that the risks are worth the possible outcome?

Determinants of FDI

Some firms will choose FDI over the other market entry options from a desire to maintain operational control. As the foregoing discussion highlights, both exporting and strategic alliances require the firm to cede a certain amount of control over their product and operations to other businesses. Firms with high manufacturing expenses will use FDI to localize production costs and build a higher level of stability into their cost structure. Still others will decide that the uniqueness of a given market, combined with high revenue potential, requires an ongoing market presence. There is the ability to reduce negative country-of-origin effect, which can be a substantial draw in some markets, and there is also the notion of "following." In most cases, "following" is not an advisable approach to business. However, in international business, your firm may decide that following the competition into a market—and learning from their mistakes—means that your firm is able to enjoy success in that market on a much larger scale through the use of FDI. Alternatively, it may be that your firm is following your client. As the sales of U.S. cars in China grows and U.S. manufacturers look toward FDI in China, so too are their suppliers. In any, or all, of these situations, the benefits to foreign direct investment can far outstrip the costs.

Summary

Although culture, and cultural differences, is frequently the part of the environment most identified with challenges in the international business environment, the physical environment is the piece often considered the most "uncontrollable." But is that really the case? As we have seen in this chapter, altering the actual physical environment may not be an option. However, like the cultural component of the international business environment, understanding exactly how the physical environment may or may not affect firm operations is an important first step. From there, a firm can then make much more informed decisions and use both market selection and market entry strategies to control for an unfavorable physical environment.

CHAPTER FOUR

The Economic Environment: A Business Perspective

Introduction

Often a discussion targeted at understanding the international business environment from the perspective of economics, and the economic environment, becomes overly focused on economic theory and policy. Clearly, these are important issues, but a theoretical approach to understanding this aspect of the environment often does not speak directly to operational challenges faced by companies. In many ways, a good understanding of the economic environment involves being able to apply economic principles and economic-based information rather than being able to derive economic "proofs" such as supply and demand curves. This chapter considers aspects of both the macro- and microeconomic environment from the perspective of practical application. It then moves to one of the driving issues for business: how can supply and demand be controlled and managed?

The Key Economic Issues in International Business

Although it could be argued that a number of economic issues are related to the international business environment that are crucial for firms to understand, these can all be traced to two basic issues: the macroeconomic questions related to the potential, or attractiveness, of a host market and the microeconomic questions that revolve around the industry and competitive dynamic of a host market. Any assessment of a host market must focus on macroeconomic characteristics of that market as it relates to the proposed role that market might play in firm operations. This means understanding how that host market is configured and how it may differ from the firm's home market—both from the perspective of possible threats as well as how that comparison may present unique opportunities for the firm. The microeconomic issues related to the competitive dynamic center around the nature of that host market in terms of the firm's ability to accomplish its stated objectives—particularly those related to revenue production—and how that competitive environment differs from the markets in which the firm currently operates.

In most cases, a host market is viewed on the basis of its potential in one of two areas. First would be its attractiveness as an operational location. The second would be its attractiveness as a revenue-generating market. This is not to imply that a firm must choose one over the other—clearly many firms will enter a host market with the express intent of both becoming more operationally efficient and, at the same time, increasing revenue production through product sales. However, these two broad categories are the most compelling reasons to enter a host market, and the underlying issues relevant to each can differ. So before trying to understand a host market from an economic perspective, it is first helpful to have an idea as to what role—operational, revenue-producing, or both—that market will likely take in the firm's overall strategy.

Assessing a host market from the perspective of its potential as an operational location means trying to ascertain the additional efficiencies the firm might expect from locating some, or all, of its operations in that market. For example, some Asian firms have realized operational advantages from locating production facilities in Mexico. These were often originally designed not to produce products for the Mexican market but rather to get closer to the U.S. market. At the same time, as the Mexican market has developed, these firms find that what was originally motivated primarily by increasing operational efficiencies has placed the firm in a market that can provide additional revenue.

A firm considering a host market as an operational location must take into account its ability to re-create the necessary processes in that market (e.g., labor costs, labor skills, infrastructure, availability of capital) along with other environmental characteristics related to operational output (e.g., taxes). On the other hand, assessing a potential host market from the perspective of a revenue-generating market means looking at consumer characteristics related to things such as demand and ability to pay, characteristics of the competition and their ability to interfere with your firm's ability to connect with those customers, and product characteristics and the role of your product in that market. With these guidelines in place, the general framework for evaluating a potential host market can be discussed.

Evaluating a Potential Host Economy

The process of evaluating a potential host economy, and the relevant issues that must be addressed in the course of that evaluation, are somewhat dependent on the anticipated role that market will play in the firm's international strategy. As we saw earlier, host markets can perform the role of an operational base, a revenue producer, or both. With that in mind, there are four basic pieces that make up the framework for evaluating a potential host market: 1) economic activity in the market, 2) demand issues, 3) resource availability, and 4) the existing economic system. An evaluation of economic activity and the economic system apply to markets that are being considered as both a possible operational location as well as a revenue generator. Demand issues, on the other hand, tend to be more identified with revenue generating activities while resource availability is associated with operational concerns.

Evaluating Economic Activity

Often a firm will look at a potential host market, and its economic activity, in the context of its own home market. This is because it is easy to use a known market as a basis of comparison with a market that may be unfamiliar. The result of such a perspective can be underestimation of the market's potential and overestimating market instability. To avoid these possible errors, the best place to start in evaluating a market's economic activity is with the source(s) of its economic development. In other words, what generates economic activity in that market and what does that mean for your firm, its products, and its operations? Markets will fall into one of three categories in terms of their economic development: primary, secondary, and tertiary. Note that each of these categories can be used to label a market in terms of its level of development, but those labels can be misleading when placed into the context of an individual firm.

Markets in which the economic activity is considered to be "primary" are frequently referred to as "lesser developed." In these markets, the economic activity is centered around agricultural and extractive (e.g., mining, timber) processes. However, it would be a mistake to conclude that these primary markets are synonymous with subsistence. It may be true that higher levels of production and service industries are not present or represent only a small portion of the overall economic activity. At the same time, this does not mean that there is no suitable demand for these types of products. Obviously, demand for products used in these primary activities could be substantial because there would be no domestic source for such products. It is also possible that an active primary economy represents an excellent location for revenue generation because of significant latent, or pent-up, demand. In this scenario, the market would be focused on these primary activities, but assuming that the activities were established and stable over time, it could mean an opportunity to provide the higher-level goods and services not be produced locally. Thus, a market that does not compare with a developed home market based on level of development could actually be a very lucrative revenue generating location. Unique opportunities might also exist from the viewpoint of a primary market as an operational location as the activities in such a market may provide access to lower cost inputs and/or increased production efficiencies.

In contrast, a secondary economy is one in which the activity involves processing the output of primary activities and producing component materials. In these markets, primary activities still take place, but there is an increased focus on using the outputs. For example, in Malaysia and Indonesia, there has always been a well-developed timber industry with much of the output being exported to use as building materials. More recently there has been an emergence of a furniture industry built around the so-called flat-pack furniture sold in discount stores in developed markets (e.g., Walmart in the United States). This type of furniture uses wood (particle board) produced from the sawdust and wood shavings that are a by-product of turning trees into lumber. As products and production in these markets becomes more sophisticated, there is the opportunity for firms and individuals to specialize, which means both more demand and the ability to pay on the part of consumers along with more operational efficiencies for firms locating in the market.

The third category of economies—the tertiary economy—is generally considered to be the most developed. These are the economies in which a significant proportion of the activity is based on the service sector. Tertiary economies are associated with the highest levels of consumer income, the broadest product selections, and the most competition. A tertiary economy is one that has the most potential but also the most risk. As we have seen in recent years, economies built around a large service sector can exhibit high levels of instability. The so-called developed markets around the globe have taken some of the biggest hits resulting in a challenging international business environment. In the past, there was a tendency to view the developed markets as high-opportunity environments—albeit with accompanying high levels of competition—where stability was only affected by the normal business cycle. In light of the past few years, it could be argued that these developed markets are the most volatile and will be hard pressed to reach the levels of growth experienced at the beginning of the new millennia. Clearly these markets continue to represent a great deal of opportunity, both as operational and revenue-generating locations, but they are not necessarily as attractive as they once were.

This leads us to the second part of analyzing a potential market's economic activity: the indicators to consider. Although there is no shortage of economic indicators that can be used to evaluate a host market, it is helpful to begin with those that have the closest relationship to the firm's basic objectives of assessing the market as an operational location and/ or as a revenue-generating location and also which can be easily used to compare one market with another. A good place to start is with indicators related to the stability and sustainability of economic activity in the market. Simple—but powerful—indicators such as the rate of inflation, level of interest rates, and stability of exchange rates, both when compared with your home currency as well as other major currencies such as the Euro along with geographically proximate currencies (e.g., the Mexican peso's relationship to the U.S. dollar), can provide an excellent foundation for understanding the stability of a potential host market.

The next step would be to contextualize these indicators of stability with the potential for sustainability—that is, addressing the matter of what the economy's growth is based on (i.e., the source of economic development discussed earlier). We then consider the rate and direction of economic growth; growth that is too rapid may be unsustainable, and growth that is essentially flat or negative (regardless of the size of the market) may represent a market in decline. However, just as it is important to put the stability of a potential host market into the context of sustainability, it is also important to put that market's current and anticipated growth into the context of your firm and its product offering(s). For any given firm, a flat or negative growth market could represent opportunity. U.S. universities have long known that the demand for MBA-level education goes up in bad economies—a lesson applied with great success by some of these institutions both in Europe and Japan. Another good example of these counterintuitive opportunities is pasta sauce. Gia Russa brand pasta sauce, produced by Summer Garden Food Manufacturing, a firm employing about 100 people in Boardman, Ohio, finds that in many markets, demand for pasta sauce goes up in bad economies because it represents a product that can "stretch" a family's food budget.

Evaluating Demand Issues

Where evaluating the economic activity in a potential host market applies to both operational and revenue-generating objectives, the evaluation of demand-related issues in the same market tends to be most important to firms that are primarily seeking to generate revenue in that market. There are three of these demand-related issues that essentially build on each other: quantity of demand, quality of demand, and quality of life. Quantity of demand establishes basic revenue-generating potential, quality of demand the possibility of developing an ongoing revenue stream, and quality of life the permanence of that revenue stream. Not all firms are able to enjoy all three levels, or types, of demand, but understanding what each represents provides insight into what needs to be achieved in a host market to enjoy the highest levels of success in terms of revenue production.

The first area to consider in evaluating the demand in a potential host market would be the actual quantity of demand. This means identifying the number of potential buyers as well as the initial ability to purchase. The indicators most often used by economists to measure quantity of demand are simple and straightforward: population and per capita income. Although these are good macro indicators for broad economic comparisons across countries, at this macro level, they are not sufficient for making sound operational decisions. For example, as noted in an earlier chapter, on the population side, China is often described as a market of tremendous demand potential simply by virtue of its overall population. What is often missed in this is that in terms of geography, China is a vast market, and much of its population is not easily accessible. Similarly, other markets are often discounted as potential revenue generators because the per capita income in significantly less than what might be considered an acceptable level in a developed, or the firm's home, market.

What must be done in accurately estimating quantity of demand in a market is to put these initial indicators of population and per capita income into context. Population, as a total number, is essentially meaningless at the firm level. What is much more valuable is to move a step further and consider population distribution and density in a market rather than the total number of people. As we've noted, the total population of China does not accurately reflect the number of individuals who cannot be effectively reached. Instead, a better means of evaluating the Chinese market would be to take into account where pockets of individuals may reside and the density of these pockets. Although this cuts down the total number of potential buyers, such an analysis shows that there are significant clusters of potential demand that can be reached effectively. Taking this approach to measuring quantity of demand not only helps to better evaluate a potential host market, it can also help to identify markets that, based solely on total population as a measure of quantity of demand, might not have been considered. The Mexican market has nowhere near the same population as that of China, but the fact that a huge number of people are concentrated into Mexico City—one of the largest cities on the planet—means that a large, accessible market does exist.

Like total population, per capita income can also be misleading. The per capita, or average, income in the United States takes into account many segments of the population that are not viable markets for many products—this average number is simply not an accurate representation of quantity of demand. The per capita income in the United States as of January 2012 was $27,773. This level of income would clearly not be sufficient to support the vast range of consumer products that are sold in the United States every day. Thus, per capita income is a poor indicator of quantity of demand. It is more helpful not to attempt to evaluate an economy based on average income. Instead, like population, we must put the income levels in that market into a more usable context.

This is where we must then turn to the second demand indicator: quality of demand. Trying to determine what is a sufficient income level in the absence of some market context is much like trying to define what it means to be "middle class." The answer is: it depends. So from a firm perspective, we must move beyond the question of how much demand exists in a market toward the question, does that demand represent any market potential? We will assume at this point that there are indications that a reasonable quantity of demand does exist in the market in question and that it can be effectively reached. Now we must consider the extent to which those consumers have the ability to pay for our product(s). The key indicators for this quality-of-demand determination are disposable income and expenditure distribution. Everyone knows that disposable income represents what is left to the individual after all other financial obligations have been met. It is all too easy to draw the conclusion that higher levels of income equate to higher levels of disposable income. Sometimes that is the case, but it is not a hard-and-fast rule. One of the primary problems in developed markets is that, although income levels are relatively high compared with all other markets in the world, high levels of financial obligations in the form of debt greatly reduce disposable income. Furthermore, the cost of living in these markets can be disproportionately high when compared with other markets. It is telling that in recent protests in New York City against the so-called 1 percent, about a third of the protesters reported incomes in excess of $200,000. In almost every other country in the world, that level of income would place those people well within the 1%. In comparison, a country that is substantially poorer than the United States—India—has the largest motion picture industry in the world. Few would argue that paying to see a movie falls well into the realm of disposable income. So where does this demand come from? Simply put, although the overall level of income in India is a fraction of that in the United States, the percentage of that income that could be viewed as "disposable" is much higher.

Evaluation of a host market's demand potential must not focus on comparisons of income levels between the home and host market but rather concentrate on how much income is available to the individual consumers. However, this does not fully address this issue of quality of demand. The firm must also be able to put its own product(s) into a context relative to priority of purchase; that is, given a choice, what do consumers in this market spend their disposable income on? This is a question of expenditure distribution. The question to answer is, where does your product fit, or potentially fit, in the buying patterns of consumers in this potential host market? As quantity of demand rises, disposable income increases, and expenditure distribution becomes more favorable for your firm's product offering because a case can be built that this particular potential market represents a revenue opportunity. There is one other possible level of demand that, although not always attainable, would solidly tip the balance in favor of any potential host market: quality-of-life level demand.

When your product reaches the level of contributing to quality of life in a particular market, it has not only been placed in a market where quality of demand exists, that quality of demand is likely to persist over time. Such a market represents a significant, sustainable source of revenue. What is easy to overlook in many developed markets—the United States included—is how the wide variety of available products contribute to a high standard of living. Over-the-counter pharmaceuticals are a prime example. Americans have the ability to treat a wide range of common ailments simply by purchasing medication at a retail store. This greatly improves quality of life but also goes largely unappreciated. Take the same types of products and price them within reach of consumers in many other markets, and they have the potential to revolutionize the standard of living. Being able to put your product in this position means much more than just brand loyalty; it means that with consumers in this market, there is a certain level of actual dependence that quickly translates into a sustainable revenue stream.

Resource Availability

When the demand issues we've discussed tend to be primarily associated with firms that seek to generate revenue in a host market, the issue of resource availability tends to be more closely associated with firms evaluating a potential host market from the perspective of its attractiveness as an operational location. As such, this evaluation can be approached sequentially, just like any manufacturing process, beginning with the availability of raw materials. As was the case in evaluating quantity of demand using total population, assessing the ability of a host market to provide necessary raw materials goes beyond their existence in that market. Availability is necessary but not sufficient. Access to these raw materials is the key issue. For example, as noted in Chapter 3, Canada has one of the largest—some experts estimate the largest—oil reserves in the world. The problem is that much of this oil resides in land close to or above the Arctic Circle where the permafrost and other natural barriers make access problematic. Just as the existence of people in a market does not constitute actionable demand, the presence of raw materials does not mean they can be effectively utilized. Access is key; without access, the raw materials are effectively useless.

Moving up a level, there is the issue of component materials. These include processed raw materials and more advanced inputs such as subassemblies. The issue here is no longer availability and accessibility; those issues would have been addressed before the market was considered as an operational location. Now the questions focus on the quality of these component materials in the processes used both in developing the components as well as those necessary to use them effectively as well. A finished product is only as good as the components and subassemblies on which it is based. A door handle represents a small piece of an automobile, but if the handle fails, the entire car can become unusable. There is frequently a temptation to locate in a market in which raw materials, components, and subassemblies are all low cost. However, the opportunity and hidden costs associated with poor product quality that might result from inferior components and subassemblies should not be overlooked. A long-term product strategy is difficult to maintain if the product itself is somehow unstable in its performance—and this performance is directly tied to these components.

Going beyond resources that represent material product inputs, there are two other resources that should be evaluated if the host market is under consideration as an operational location. The first such resource that can, and often is, ineffectively assessed is labor. The temptation is to seek out markets that have low labor costs. Unfortunately, like the component issue, firms can fail to recognize that the old adage "you get what you pay for" can apply to sourcing local labor in a host market. Firms must go beyond just labor costs and look to the long term. Setting up operations in a host market is expensive and time-consuming—and because of these factors firms will anticipate utilizing these facilities over an extended period of time. This means that the ability of the workforce to "grow" becomes important; employees should be evaluated not just along the lines of wage expenses but also from the perspective of education, skills, experience, and overall ability to adjust, adapt, and be effectively used in a wide variety of tasks and activities. These represent the foundation of a workforce that can grow as the operational needs of your firm change over time.

Which brings us to the last resource that may be problematic in a host market but that firms nonetheless require for operations: capital availability. From the point of view of a home market, capital availability may simply mean access to the source, whether through financing or investment. In a host market, this concept of availability can be more complicated and extend to areas such as currency conversion, the ability to move capital in and out of the market, government involvement in the capital market, along with myriad other possible restrictions related not only to capital creation but also to its use. Firms coming from developed, essentially "free" markets can easily forget that the flow of capital is a primary means for governments to control any economy and that the operations of a non-domestic firm are an easy target for restrictions on capital flow. This then leads to the fourth, and final, area that must be taken into account when evaluating a potential host economy: the economic system itself.

The Host Market Economic System

Evaluating the host market economic system closes the loop of the process. At this juncture, we are not evaluating the economic system from the perspective of its ideology; that is considered in Chapter 5. Instead, whether the firm seeks to engage the prospective host market as an operational location or as a revenue generator, this involves an analysis of the government's role in the economy in areas where the firm and the host government could come in direct operational contact—and perhaps conflict. There are three areas in which such a scenario could arise. These would be active government ownership in your firm's industry, active government participation in resource allocation, and the overall role of government in the economy (i.e., facilitator vs. provider).

When a host government assumes firm ownership in your industry it becomes a direct competitor. On one hand, this is particularly disturbing as governments tend to have much larger resource bases on which to operate, are not necessarily held accountable for poor performance, and have a distinct advantage when it comes to the interpretation of laws and regulations governing the industry. However, it is equally plausible that, in an industry where the government plays an active ownership role, lucrative opportunities are created. The bottom line is that governments, although they may have access to large quantities of resources, are generally not terribly effective and efficient in operating at the firm level. To a large extent, this is due to the underlying reason the government assumes control in the first place: to fulfill a social responsibility. When this is the case, unlike private firms, performance is not measured using traditional business benchmarks but by the quantity of product provided. The result is available product but not always of the highest quality, creating opportunities for firms at the high end to carve out a premium niche.

There are numerous examples both in goods manufacturing (e.g., automobiles) and in the service sector (e.g., national health services) in which governments, in an attempt to ensure overall economic well-being through the provision of jobs, universal health care, and other desirable social objectives—achieve these goals but create market space for those firms willing to provide higher-quality products. In every developed market with government-provided health care, there is a lucrative parallel market for specialized treatments offered by private providers. Alternatively, one can consider the case of British Leyland, a UK government-owned car manufacturer from years past. The government's motivation in operating this company was to provide manufacturing jobs, not well-designed and manufactured automobiles. The resulting inefficiencies meant that the British auto industry became dominated by nondomestic producers. When the government takes an active ownership role, it can be intimidating, but the best firms are able to recognize the potential in such an environment.

On the other hand, the government in the host market may take an active role in the allocation of resources in your industry. This may result in host firms receiving competitive advantage, such as government subsidies. In a sense, when this situation arises, the government essentially becomes an indirect owner—or at least partial owner—in the local industry. Again, like the situation in which direct government ownership leads to inefficiencies, government allocation of resources also creates potential dysfunction within an industry. This becomes problematic when, unlike straight government firm ownership, local firms are much more likely to seek to use these resources to maximize profit and competitive advantage rather than fulfill a social role in the economy. A good example of this would be the agriculture industry in France, which has always been heavily subsidized by the government. The local producers use these subsidies to gain "unnatural" profits and keep the market essentially closed off to nondomestic providers. The negative ramifications of such a competitive environment cannot be ignored and should be fully investigated before entering this type of economy because it could represent a real, long-term competitive disadvantage for the outside firm.

The last area to consider is the overall role of government in the economy. That is, does the government perform the role of facilitator or provider? Governments all play some role in any economy. As we have discussed, when they assume the role of provider (e.g., take ownership within an industry), this means space at the bottom is often crowded out by the government's activities, but this, in turn, can create space at the top that is more profitable. But what does it mean when the government is viewed as a facilitator? From a company's point of view, government "facilitation" can be seen as an impediment to operations (e.g., industry regulations), but for a nondomestic firm, these types of facilitation can be a blessing. When governments become involved in facilitating industries, they can create a false or imperfect structure. Where the advantage comes to nondomestic firms in is this very structure. Having a clear, structured economic environment can mean less uncertainty, which creates a more advantageous planning environment. In the end, the inefficiencies created by government involvement can be overridden by the advantages of a more structured, certain marketplace. Just as in the previous discussions regarding economic activity, demand issues, and resource availability, understanding a host market's economic system in terms of government's role means placing the activities into the local context and your firm's operations rather than simply comparing against your firm's home market.

Barriers to Operating Across Economies: Trade Restrictions

Types

Having now considered how best to evaluate a potential host market, we turn next to challenges that could present themselves if a firm enters a given market. These can be characterized one of two ways: as barriers to operating across markets (i.e., between home and host markets) and barriers to operating within a specific market (most notably the competition). Although they have been addressed to some extent in another chapter, let's again take a look at the various types of trade restrictions and how they present challenges to operating across markets by impeding the flow of products.

The first category of trade barrier would be a tariff. Tariff can come in different forms (e.g., percent of invoice, specific duty), but they operate as an overt tax. Obviously, no firm (or government) wants to pay additional taxes on their products—especially as a direct cost of entering another market. However, as a trade barrier, tariffs are typically viewed as the most acceptable from both a firm and a government perspective. Because they are specific and transparent, there is much less uncertainty associated with tariffs than the other forms of trade restrictions. Throughout this book, one of the main themes is the need to reduce uncertainty to be successful in international business. The ability to clearly identify exactly how the flow of product might be adversely affected when moving between markets makes it much easier to develop appropriate strategies—or opt out of operating in that particular market. The overt nature of tariffs also makes it more feasible to enlist the assistance of the firm's home government in reducing or eliminating these barriers. Like firms, governments prefer to deal with obstacles that are in clear sight—it helps to identify the best trading partners and create a more effective international trade policy.

Unfortunately, not all trade restrictions that a firm might face are as open and obvious as tariffs. The next category is what are known as nontariff/quantitative barriers (e.g., quotas, voluntary export restraints [VERs]). As the name implies, these are not taxes on products that enter a market but rather limits on the number of products that can enter that market. The problem created by this form of trade barrier is subjectivity in the definition of what does, or does not, fall within the definition of products subject to these limits. Tariffs tend to be relatively straightforward to deal with; quotas introduce a higher level of uncertainty. Changes in which products are subjected to some form of quota can be effected, quite literally, overnight. It is not uncommon for these changes to be within the authority of relatively low-level government officials, and administering these changes is often quite simple because they do not require any alteration in a transactional process. One day a firm's product may not be limited by an existing quota, the next the flow of product is significantly constrained. In a nontariff/quantitative environment, uncertainty related to the level of product flow over time comes into question. A firm involved in, or evaluating, a host market where such trade restrictions exist should take into account the potentially unstable nature of product flow into the market.

The one advantage, if it can be called an advantage, of nontariff/quantitative trade barriers is that they are at least focused on the product with the express goal of limiting product flow—they are an obvious restriction.

The third category of trade restrictions is not as clear-cut; indeed, it can often take the form of a trade barrier masquerading as another type of government policy. These are known as nontariff/nonquantitative barriers. They can range from government subsidies, to procurement policies, customs and administrative procedures, down to simple standards. Their intention may be to keep out, or limit, nondomestic products, or they may be in place to otherwise regulate the market, but they then have the secondary effect of limiting the flow of products. In either case, the result for firms is the same: a trade restriction exists.

Justifications

While a global economy exists, there remains this problem of the market imperfections caused by trade restrictions. Any time the flow of goods is impeded, costs rise and the attractiveness of operating in the restricted market drops. Unfortunately, although such barriers prevent free trade and are counter to the concept of a globalized economy, they do exist. When they present themselves as a problem, it is important for firms to understand how that host market defends their existence. This understanding provides insight into not only the best means of managing these impediments, thereby reducing the negative impact, but also the permanency of their existence. So, in a global economy, what are the justifications for the existence of trade restrictions?

One that is frequently encountered in both developed and developing markets is the "national defense" justification. Governments—the United States included—will control the flow of goods in and out of the market if those goods are viewed as being crucial to national defense. For example, the U.S. government is sensitive to the movement of all manner of technology because virtually all types have some national defense application (e.g., remote controlled "toys" could be a model airplane or an air force drone). As long as the product remains relevant to national defense, the firm's ability to move it in and out of other markets will be limited. In such cases, this means a greatly reduced number of potential markets—likely only those with close and enduring policy ties with the home market—and any product movement will be closely monitored, resulting in additional time and resource expenditures. Being subject to trade restrictions based on a national defense justification is not always an obvious call; there are many cases in which industries are classified as important to national defense that are not necessarily intuitive (e.g., the U.S. shoe industry was at one time considered to be vital to national defense).

The second category of trade restriction justification is the protection of an infant industry. This is likely to be less permanent than the national defense justification, but it can effectively close off a potential market for a substantial period of time. These are most common in emerging and newly emerged markets. Furthermore, they are also most commonly associated with higher-level manufactured goods that would have the potential to facilitate further economic development both within the market and as an export to other developed markets. Korea is an example of a nation that historically has protected markets earmarked as important for the long-term success of the economy (e.g., silicon chip production). The rationale is simple—without competitive safeguards, the new firms in these markets would not survive when pitted against established nondomestic firms. Protecting the industry allows it to move up the learning curve at a faster rate. However, at some point if the government seeks to export this product in any quantity, it is more than likely that the trade restrictions will be removed based on demands from the product's destination market(s).

The remaining justifications are, perhaps, easier to manage proactively. The first, trade restrictions designed to ensure "fair" competition, are often a synonym for host-market firm inefficiencies. For example, tomato producers in the United States have had difficulty competing with Mexican tomato importers in terms of costs and profits. In this situation, the result is often a trade "restriction" that benefits the nondomestic firm, such as a price floor (minimum price), which is essentially a mandated price increase to meet the margin requirements of the local firms. In the end, the nondomestic firm may simply enjoy higher profits at the expense of local consumers. Regardless of how this type of barrier might affect your firm, the key to managing the "fair competition" restrictions proactively is to take steps to demonstrate your firm's willingness to compete "fairly."

The second, more manageable justification is one of retaliation. This can be the result of home government policies (e.g., subsidies) but is often based on a claim of "dumping." The classic definition of dumping is selling below cost of production to drive out competition. This is a hard case to prove. Instead, host-market governments—and the firms they represent—will use surrogate indicators of dumping, most notably a comparison of price in the home market versus the host market or comparisons of pricing differences across a range of markets. When the price of your product is less in the host market(s) than at home, there is an immediate red flag because it is generally accepted that the cost of doing business across markets is higher than operating within a single market. This is true but it may be that extenuating circumstances (e.g., high taxes) exist in your home market to which your product is not subject in the host market. Irrespective of the underlying cause of the price differential, when substantial price differences exist, your firm may be at risk for trade restrictions.

Barriers to Operating within an Economy: Competition

It would be easy to separate any discussion of the economic environment and the competition. On one hand, many of the economic issues we have covered to this point fall into the category of "macro" related topics that establish the lay of the land in a nondomestic market. On the other hand, the competitive environment and the firms that comprise that environment operate to at least some extent in the same economic environment as your firm. However, remember that we are committed to understanding the economic environment from a business perspective, not that of an economist. This means we must certainly take into account these overall macro aspects of a market but also attend to the micro, or industry-related, as well. Our take on establishing a good understanding of the economic environment is that we must account for anything that can impede not just the attractiveness of the market and the flow of goods and revenues in and out of that market but also anything that could impede a firm's ability to complete these transactions. By definition, that is exactly the threat posed by competing firms, and therefore understanding the competition becomes essential to understanding the economic environment of any international market.

Sources of Competition and Source Advantage

A good starting point in developing this understanding is to identify the primary source of your firm's actual competition. At first blush it would be logical to assume that in another market, the most crucial source of competition would be local firms. If the market has been judged to be a serious market of opportunity, then, by extension, a serious weakness exists in the local competition. The next logical conclusion is that, because the local firms are somehow lacking, there is no significant competition. This is a dangerous assumption to make. Not all competitive advantages are derived from market and product-based characteristics, and not all serious competition will necessarily originate from the local, or host, market.

Certainly, host-market firms can be a source of competitive threat. Some of this may be related to market awareness and brand equity. In both consumer and business products, a level of familiarity can cover a variety of firm and product deficiencies. Both types of customers simply tend to prefer certainty—however potentially flawed—to the uncertainty and risks associated with trying new products. Additionally, there may be other issues that give the host firms an edge. The country-of-origin effect (drawing conclusions—potentially both negative and positive—about a firm and a product based solely on the perception of the country to which they are associated) can be the basis for host firm competitive advantage. In exploring the true sources of any firm's competition in a market, the best place to start is with host firms but to move beyond the aspects that represent direct firm and product advantages to anything within the context of that market that might give these host firms an edge.

The second potential source of substantial competition would be other "home" firms. Although some firms may be able to exercise a "first-mover" advantage when entering a new market, it is rare for any firm to have an extended, exclusive competitive advantage. If a firm from one particular home market identifies a host market of opportunity, it frequently follows that its home market competitors follow suit. However, of the three sources of competition in an international market, other home market firms may pose the lowest threat. Where firms from other markets represent a certain level of uncertainty in terms of how they operate, firms from the home market are relatively "known" quantities. This does not completely remove them as a threat in the new market, but—assuming these firms represent a significant competitive force—it does provide a clearer picture of how the competitive landscape might look and what can be expected from those competing firms.

The third category of firms would be those from other markets—neither host nor home. For example over the years in markets such as South America, General Motors has found its largest competitors have been Volkswagen and the various Japanese carmakers. Sometimes, like other home market firms, these are reasonably known quantities in their competitive behavior. However, it may be that in a new market these firms enjoy advantages to which your firm does not have access. These "source advantages" are often associated with host-market firms such as subsidies or other government-based assistance only available to local companies. But it could be equally true that policy arrangements between the host-market government and their own home government could result in these firm's enjoying additional benefits such as a reduced level of trade barriers, controlled exchange rates, or ease of revenue repatriation. Understanding the source of competition in a new market is vital to anticipating how those firms will compete, and a large part of this is understanding the advantages available to them based on their market of origin.

Assessing Competitive Advantage

Once the primary source of competition—and any attending source advantages—can be identified, the next step in understanding the competition in a new market involves assessing individual firms and their specific competitive strengths and weaknesses. This starts with the basic questions of who is the competition now and who will be the competition in the future. This may seem superficial, but remember the firms with which your firm competes are determined not by industry type or product classification, but by your customers. This means conducting a value-oriented assessment from the customer's perspective. Product uses change from one market to the next, customers seek out different service and personnel values, and the role of branding an image might be different from one market to the next; likewise, there is the potential for your customers to identify product substitutes (i.e., competitors). Firms that adopt the notion that the competitive set can be defined using strictly industry and product types run the risk of misidentifying their competition.

Once competitors have been identified, it is necessary to determine the importance those competitors attach to that particular market. No firm has unlimited resources. Therefore, establishing the competition's level of investment and expenditures in a market can go a long way in determining whether they will be actively fighting for market share or, alternatively, be willing to cede competitive advantage in favor of other markets to which they attach higher priority. A good example of this varying competitive advantage is the interplay over the years between Coke and Pepsi in markets around the world. Coke has historically been one of the top, most recognized brand names worldwide. This type of brand equity is invaluable when entering a new market. However, brand recognition is generally not enough to secure long-term market share. Coke now sees some markets as high priorities because the initial product introduction based on high levels of brand equity was not followed up with additional investment. In these markets, Pepsi has been able to gain long-term competitive advantage through additional, relatively modest investment spread out over time that has overcome Coke's stronger brand. The lesson is simple: even when there appears to be a distinct advantage, this must be actively managed. Failure to do so can give what might appear to be lesser firms the ability to secure a dominant role in any given market.

At this point, your firm should have an idea of its most likely individual competitors. Now it is time to consider their specific strengths and weaknesses. Identifying strengths is typically straightforward. No firm wants to hide its strengths; indeed, these are the very things that will be openly promoted to gain customers. This means that the basis on which the firm believes it can beat others is easily established. Analyzing any company's product positioning strategy and presentation in the market quickly establishes the basis for how that firm intends to beat its competitors. The grocery industry in Great Britain is a good example of this: Tesco's presents itself as the low-cost alternative, Sainsbury's uses a combination of value and quality, and Waitrose markets itself as a specialty-quality brand. When Walmart began to aggressively move into the grocery market in the United

Kingdom through its Asda stores, it knew the primary competitor would be Tesco's based on Tesco's focus on more for less. Directing resources at beating Tesco's has been relatively successful, and currently these four companies account for more than 80 percent of the market share of the grocery industry in England.

Identifying the competition's exploitable weaknesses, on the other hand, is not quite as easy. No firm advertises its shortcomings. One approach would be to engage in a market research program focused on uncovering weaknesses, but this would likely involve substantial amounts of time and other resources. Given that both strengths and weaknesses are essentially perceptions in the marketplace, a faster and more effective approach would be to manage those perceptions; in other words, create exploitable weaknesses in the mind of the consumers. This is not an exercise in deceit or unethical behavior. Rather, this is a recognition that even if objective, factual weaknesses can be identified, it may be that the marketplace simply doesn't care. Instead of spending time and money trying to specify things which may or may not be viewed as relevant, it is more efficient to "direct" the market's attention toward what your firm and product can be considered to do particularly well, with the implied message that your competition falls short in these vital areas and therefore has a weaker offering. In the end, strengths and weaknesses are based on what the market thinks it knows, not necessarily on actual facts.

Maintaining Competitive Advantage

Although gaining any kind of competitive advantage in the international marketplace is a significant challenge, it is all for nothing if that advantage cannot be maintained. This means adopting a conscious, long-term strategic approach—something that most firms have a real problem doing. Every successful company, and even many less-than-successful companies, engage in what is often referred to as "strategic planning." Unfortunately, it is often the case that the resulting plans look less like a long-term vision and more like an annual sales forecast. This temptation to focus only on short-term profits means that the average life span of firms in the United States and Europe is estimated to be about 12 years. However, there are notable examples of companies whose willingness to look beyond the annual report has allowed them to survive and thrive for centuries (e.g., the Japanese firm Sumitomo is 400 years old). The first requirement in maintaining competitive advantage is to operate strategically and manage over the long term. The demands of shareholders and other constituents can make this problematic. However, considering the time, effort, and financial resources required for success in international markets, any failure to operate with a long-term vision is likely to doom international operations before they even have a chance.

An extension of this need to manage with a long-term perspective is the need to proactively manage those key individuals who comprise the organization. The average tenure of executives both in the United States and Europe at any given firm is incredibly short—by some estimates, less than three years. It is impossible to maintain any semblance of competitive advantage if those at the highest level of decision making in a firm are constantly changing. The best firms not only are able to find top-quality managers, they are also able to nurture and retain these individuals. An organization is only as good as the people who comprise it, and consistency in that composition is essential for success.

The final piece is to be prepared for the unknown. The best firms—especially those that maintain long-term success outside of their domestic market—are the ones that are prepared to move quickly. It is impossible to anticipate all potential threats, but it is possible to engage actively in contingency planning and threat management. Firms that do this on a regular basis find that even if a particular scenario is new, the fact that the company has practiced dealing with "surprises" means it is better able to cope effectively. This exercise of trying to see into the future can also provide a basis for first-mover advantage when changes in the market do occur. For example, at one point, firms in the UK brewing industry had developed business models involving new product lines in the anticipation that cannabis could be legalized. To this point, that hasn't happened—and there has been no decision that those firms would become involved with this particular product—but it is a good example of how firms can be visionaries in their attempt to maintain competitive advantage.

This brings us to the final issue in the discussion of competitive advantage: what will the competition do in the future? This can be a tricky issue. When the competition takes a bold new step, there is always the temptation to follow. After all, any change in direction on the part of the competition might mean losing your firm's edge in the market. When these situations arise, it is absolutely important to remember that your competition probably has no more ability to see into the future than your firm. It can be dangerous to blindly follow the competition but also very tempting when operating in the uncertain environment of international business. Rather than falling prey to this temptation, consider the ramifications of the competition's new course. For example, when Goodyear opted to move beyond its established dealer network and sell tires in retail outlets such as Walmart, companies such as Michelin could have panicked based on the increased access to such a large number of customers. The alternative view was that Goodyear might be able to move more tires but would end up diluting their brand image, which would result in reduced margins and fewer profits—which is exactly what happened. Never assume that your competition has a crystal ball and can see into the future. A better course is to develop—and adhere to—your own long-term strategic plan.

Summary

In assessing the economic aspects of the international business environment, take a practical, rather than a purely theoretical, approach. In this chapter, we have explored the key economic issues that firms must deal with in the course of their international operations. The discussion then turned to evaluating a potential host economy—its economic activity, demand-related issues, resource availability, and market system. From there, barriers to operating across markets (i.e., trade restrictions) were considered. Finally, barriers to operating within an economy (i.e., competition) and important issues such as assessing and maintaining competitive advantage were addressed.

CHAPTER FIVE

The Political and Legal Environment: Dealing with New Markets and New Rules

Introduction

Apart from the cultural environment, the political and legal environment of international business is perhaps the most difficult for businesses to understand. In large part, this is because, like culture, the political and legal environment comprises elements that are frequently viewed as being beyond the ability of companies to manage, they are not traditionally associated with "business," and, with the exception of trade barriers that result from the political process, not always considered within the context of firm operations. In this chapter, we dispel some of these myths, particularly those related to the inability of an individual firm to manage this part of the international business environment.

Firms that actively monitor and participate in the political environment are far more likely to succeed in their international endeavors. However, this is an aspect of international business that has received much less attention than, say, dealing with cultural differences. There may be many reasons for this, but two seem to stand out. First, there is a sense in the business community in many countries that firms that are seen to be proactive in dealing with the political environment are somehow breaking the rules of ethical business practices. Yet these same companies pay taxes and are affected by the political process just as individuals in a country are. This being the case, it would seem to be foolish of firms not to pay close attention to the political environment—as long as the firm is ethical and responsible in its approach, it has every right to participate in the political process. The second reason, perhaps more telling especially for international firms, is that in the somewhat limited research available on this topic, there is a clear sense from businesses that being active in the political environment can provide a real competitive edge in international operations. Therefore, because our goal is to gain a deeper understanding of all aspects of the international business environment, we would be remiss if we did not spend some time discussing both the intricacies of the political and legal environment of international business, but also some ways an individual firm can go about dealing with this part of the environment in the course of its activities in other markets.

What Is the "Political Environment"?

Virtually all of this chapter focuses on the political environment. This is not to say that the legal environment is not an important influencer on international business; clearly it is. At the same time, there are good reasons for firms to focus their efforts more on the political rather than the legal environment. These are primarily due to the fundamental difference between the "political" and the "legal." The political environment is the decision-making process through which laws, regulations, and so forth that impact international business are derived. The legal environment—those laws and regulations—is the outcome of the political process. Although this process can be managed at some level, and if it cannot be managed its outcomes can be anticipated and planned for, the legal environment is an area of international operations in which the firm can only really adapt.

Truly proactive firms will become involved in the political process to, as best as possible, control either the outcome of the process or place themselves in a position in which they can adjust and adapt to the outcome before the competition. Thus, our discussion focuses on the political rather than the legal environment. There is a second good reason to spend more time on the political aspect: knowledge of the legal environment is highly specialized. The smart firm does not attempt to go too far into any aspect of the legal environment—domestic or nondomestic—without the assistance of an attorney. At the end of the chapter, we touch on some of the important issues in the legal environment of international business, but any legal issues that the firm may encounter should be referred to a knowledgeable professional.

A good working definition is the best way to begin our exploration of the political environment and its relationship with international business.

So what is the political environment? For our purposes, the political environment is all nonmarket individuals, institutions, and organizations within a nation-state that influence the ability of a firm to operate in that market. The crucial piece of this definition is the term "nonmarket." As we look deeper into the political environment, it will mean looking outside of those influencers of success associated with the marketplace—customers, competitors, and suppliers, and so on. Whereas customers, competitors, and the various members of a supply chain can directly influence success or failure in the market, the nonmarket players can assist or inhibit the ability of the firm to achieve its goals in another market. Later on in this chapter, we look in much greater detail at how this can happen and what firms may be able to do to counter political threats. But for now our focus is on identifying these nonmarket players. From there, we move to the context in which they operate (i.e., the nation-state) and finally how their power and influence is exerted.

The influencers in the nonmarket, political environment can be characterized as either government or nongovernment influencers. Government influencers—politicians and civil servants—play the respective roles of creating and enforcing laws and regulations that impact firms operating within their country. Nongovernment influencers—opinion leaders and special interest groups—both directly and indirectly influence the political process through which these laws and regulations are derived. In a host market, understanding the composition of that country's political environment is the crucial first step. Once the firm has a reasonably clear picture of which of these influencers may, or may not, be significant and the best means to interact with them, it can begin to develop strategies for how best to manage and operate within that unique political environment.

In addition to determining the extent to which each of these influencers may play a role in the political environment of a host market, it is also prudent to take time to consider how each, in turn, may be influenced or managed by entities, such as businesses, that exist outside of that environment. In countries where politicians play an important role in the political process, understanding the role and functioning of elections and election cycles is important. Note: we are assuming that politicians are elected officials. Clearly that is not always the case, but we deal with the distinction between "permanent" and "elected" politicians later when we discuss sources of authority within nations. For now, our attempt to understand the political environment and how it works starts with the influence exerted by politicians as elected officials. In this type of situation, understanding that the politician's focus is on maintaining relevance by holding office and that office can only be held through success in the election process, helps a firm to focus its efforts in interacting and managing these officials—and by extension the political process. Civil servants, on the other hand, are generally not affected by an election cycle. Rather, their motivation is often centered on maintaining relevance through the accumulation and use of authority. When civil servants become an important component of the political "mix," then any firm resources that can be directed at assisting a key civil servant(s) in obtaining and administering authority enables the firm to manage this element of the political environment.

Whereas the government influencers are all about creating and enforcing laws and regulations, the nongovernment pieces of the political environment influence the process. Opinion leaders are individuals whose views inspire large groups to follow them. What sets these opinions leaders apart from any other individuals—after all, everybody has an opinion—is their ability to voice that opinion. Without "voice" (e.g., ongoing access to media) the opinion leader becomes irrelevant. When these individuals become a prominent force within a country, anything a firm can do to give them "voice" will help further its ability to manage the opinion leader's influence of the political process. Similarly, the special interest group also requires access to media to maintain relevance, but not quite to the same extent as the opinion leader. This is because the special interest group is not created around an individual but rather around a "cause." Provided that cause is a legitimate and ongoing issue within the society, the level of media access necessary to keep it in the public's consciousness may not extend beyond reminders. However, a firm can still attach itself to a special interest group with an eye to managing its influence on the political process by helping to further the cause that led to the creation of the group in the first place.

Understanding that the political environment is made up of more than just politicians—and that coming to some determination as to the composition, or mix, of these various influencers—government and nongovernment—along with what is most likely to motivate these individuals, organizations, and institutions is the beginning of an understanding of the unique political environment contained in a host market. The next step is to take into account the place where these influencers operate. Throughout this book, the "place" where these influencers operate is known as the market, host country, or similar terms. It is also known as the "nation-state."

The Political Environment and the Nation-State

Understanding the political environment in the context of international business means understanding the role the nation-state plays in defining the political environment. The political process and all the activities associated with the political environment, take place within the boundaries of a market or country (aka "nation-state"). This may seem an obvious—even superficial—statement until we peel apart the characteristics of a nation-state and what these mean to international business. First, a nation-state exists within a defined geographic territory. This means that the processes and controls are only relevant within a finite operational area, and what might work well in one country does not necessarily apply in another. As we saw in our discussion of exporting, it is a mistake to assume that what works well in one market will work equally well in another. Because the political environment is configured around government and nongovernment influencers—and this configuration can easily change from one country to another—any approach to addressing problems that emerge from the political process must be placed into the context of the defined nation-state.

A second characteristic of a nation-state is sovereignty. This means that the government influencers of the political environment have recognized authority to develop and administer laws and regulations within the country's defined geographic territory. Legitimate sovereignty (i.e., recognized authority that establishes the nation-state) has both an internal and an external aspect. Internal sovereignty means that the government influencers of the political environment have a recognized authority to exercise power within the defined boundaries. An absence of this internal sovereignty means that no functional nation-state exists, as was the case in several countries that experienced the so-called Arab Spring in 2011. There is also the need for external sovereignty, which involves the mutual recognition on the part of other nations of an individual state's internal sovereignty. This is also necessary for a stable, functioning nation-state to exist; witness Iraq in 2001 before the coalition invasion.

As the defined geographic territory establishes the relevant boundaries for a particular political environment, the need for internal and external sovereignty establishes the existence of a stable and functioning political process. The third characteristic of the nation-state is power monopoly. Power monopoly refers to the ability of the government members of the political environment to exercise exclusive power within its borders. This does not mean an absence of recourse if a nondomestic firm finds itself in political or legal difficulties in its host market; rather, this power monopoly means that the process is defined and ultimately controlled by the political process in the host market—the local authorities have the final word. Just as understanding the importance and composition of the various influencers of the political environment creates a picture of the nature of that environment, the three characteristics of a nation-state help provide a picture of what a legitimate market looks like in terms of the political process. The third key element is to understand the various means through which power may be exerted within a nation-state.

Sources of Authority in the Nation-State

Having a clear picture of the means through which power is exerted in a nation-state helps one to understand both the stability of that market as well as the role of the different influencers (government and nongovernment) in the market. Ultimately the process through which laws and regulations are created and enforced is significant in that it brings together the question of the roles of the various influencers and the means through which internal sovereignty might be both influenced and exerted. Generally speaking, there are five frameworks through which power is exerted within a market: 1) a traditional monarchy, 2) a constitutional monarchy, 3) a theocracy/quasi-theocracy, 4) a constitutional republic, and 5) a communist state.

Within a traditional monarchy, absolute sovereignty is vested in a hereditary ruler. Traditional monarchies are becoming rare around the world, but some still persist in countries important to the world economy such as Saudi Arabia. Because political power resides within the structure of the ruling family, in a traditional monarchy, three of the four types of influencers do not exist in any significant mainstream form. Politicians, opinion leaders, and special interests groups either simply do not exist or are not part of the mainstream political process. This leaves the civil servants, who wield a great deal of power because it is their task to implement and enforce the mandated laws and regulations. The attention of the ruling families in the remaining traditional monarchies around the world is focused on maintaining power—which means controlling and/or marginalizing competing political parties, individuals with opposing views, or any group that threatens their power. Thus, civil servants are in the uniquely powerful position of implementing policy.

In a constitutional monarchy, such as Great Britain, a hereditary monarch serves as the head-of-state while democratic institutions (e.g., Parliament) perform governmental duties and manage the political process. In this type of political environment, all four influencers can play an important role. The fundamentally important difference that separates the constitutional monarchy from the other types of nation-states is the unique role of the monarch. It is tempting to characterize monarchs in this system as "figureheads," but this is overly simplistic. The role of the monarch in a constitutional monarchy is almost as a special type of opinion leader.

The ruling monarch—and his or her family—represents a personification of the national identity in many cases. Anything such monarchs might attach themselves to, or be identified with, is virtually sanctioned as being "approved" within the market. For example, one of the most sought-after endorsements within the retail trade in England is having the right to display the Royal Warrant, which is a mark signifying they have provided goods or services to the Royal Family for at least five years. Being closely identified with the monarch or his or her activities can reduce many political problems for a nondomestic firm.

A theocracy, or quasi-theocracy, is, from the perspective of Western firms, a very different form of government and political environment. In most Western democracies, indeed in many countries around the world, there is a clear separation of church and state. In a theocracy/quasi-theocracy, church and state are pushed together. In a pure theocracy (e.g., Afghanistan under the Taliban), laws are based on religious texts and enforced based on religious prescriptions. Currently no truly pure theocracy exists. However, other nations do have what is referred to as a quasi-theocracy (e.g., Iran). Here, religious leaders assume the role of a dominant force in the political process. All the other influencers—government and nongovernment—may operate to some degree, but all are controlled within the context of the dominant religion. In this type of environment, it is absolutely crucial that a firm and its products not violate—or even give the impression of being counter to—the established religious beliefs and values because this can quickly create a source of political risk for the firm.

The constitutional republic is a familiar political environment for firms from developed markets. In the constitutional republic, sovereignty is "codified" in a basic document(s) (e.g., the U.S. Constitution, Bill of Rights) with all laws and regulations expected to adhere to the tenets of the principles and guidelines contained in these documents. Typically, all four influencers are represented and play an important role in the political process. On one hand, this means the constitutional republic—with its heavy emphasis on guiding principles and not individuals—is a stable political environment. At the same time, because the political process is carried out by individuals—particularly elected individuals—there is an element of instability associated with the constitutional republic. The fundamental principles that *guide* the process remain unchanged, but the people who *implement* the process—and the resulting laws and regulations—can change on a regular basis through the electoral process. It is important that firms involved in a market in which the political process is based on the principles of a constitutional republic recognize the paradoxical nature of the political environment.

The communist state represents a special case in defining the nature of power and authority in a nation-state. In a communist state, sovereignty rests with the party and is exercised through a core group of politically strong leaders. Politicians and civil servants merge into one, while opinion leaders and special interest groups become marginalized—at times to the point of being outside of the political process (i.e., illegal). In some ways, operating in a communist state is similar to that of a traditional monarchy. Anything the firm can do to further the power of the status quo will be viewed favorably, and the power of civil servants, at all levels, is substantial. At the present time, the only relevant communist state that currently exists is China, and the role of imported goods in building up the quality of life has been a serious component of the government's policies to maintain power—a real advantage for nondomestic firms in China that are equipped to work within the confines of the rules established by the party.

Regardless of the means through which power is exerted in the market in which the firm has chosen to operate, it is incumbent on the firm to have an understanding of the type of nation-state the market is and, by extension, what that means for the balance of influencers on the political process. The next issue to understand as we move toward how to develop strategies and tactics for managing the political environment is what specific aspects of the political environment can have a direct impact on international/host-market operations. From there, we will look at the resulting environmental factors contributing to political risk, the manifestation of that risk (i.e., political threats), and how firms can deal with these threats.

The Political Environment and International Business

Not every host market is necessarily associated with high levels of political risk. As we established in our discussion of culture, differences do not always constitute threats. Furthermore, depending on the firm and its product(s), some may find a market particularly challenging when it comes to political risk (e.g., financial services, health care) and others do not (e.g., business-to-business manufacturing). Being able to identify the characteristics of a market more likely to have higher levels of political risk regardless of product or industry is the logical first step as we move from describing the political environment toward specific types of political threats and how firms can deal with these threats.

These host-market characteristics involve both how the government and political environment are organized as well as how government is administered (i.e., government policies and the means through which policy is implemented). A good place to start in gauging the potential for political risk would be by looking at how political power and authority are administered in the market. This is about identifying the overall ideology of politics in the market (i.e., sources of authority). In other words, this is about looking more deeply at the actual organization of the political environment and the structure for the exercise of authority. It would be easy to assume that any political environment is singular in it organization, but that is rarely the case. Although there may be a single set of principles, such as a constitution, that guide the creation of laws and regulations, it is unlikely that one single federal system exists for the actual creation and enforcement of all laws and regulations which impact international business activities.

Understanding the division of power in a market is essential to understanding the overall political environment. For example, in the United States, laws and regulations that affect business exist at the federal, state, and local levels. This means a firm, depending on its product and market entry strategy, may have to deal with a variety of rules for getting its product to the consumer. Consider how this would affect a firm selling imported beer in the United States. To begin with, there are the various federal laws and regulations related to importing any product, and alcohol specifically, into the U.S. market. Then there are state laws related to where the product can be sold. Finally, there are local laws stipulating when the product can be sold. Being able to understand the division of power in a given market specifically as it relates to your firm's strategies and product has a great deal to do with the probability of success in that market.

Related to this is the issue of "law and order" in the society. Firms used to operating in the traditional developed markets around the world (e.g., the United States, Europe) frequently make the assumption that if laws and regulations exist, they are enforced. This is not always the case. As the global marketplace has rapidly expanded, many countries have felt compelled to, at least on the surface, create a market environment that is similar to the developed nations they hope to emulate. One of the quickest ways to accomplish this is through the creation of a similar legal environment. However, enforcing the resulting laws and regulations may be problematic, whether due to a lack of resources or expertise or simply a lack of commitment. Technology firms, for example, have discovered that in many markets, the presence of rules protecting intellectual property in no way ensures their property will actually be protected from copyright and patent infringement as the recent experience of Apple and its retail stores—real and fake—in China demonstrates.

On the policy side, there are a number of aspects of politics and political policy that can lead to political risk for nondomestic firms. Something that U.S. firms in particular find challenging is the extent to which host-country governments can be direct participants in the marketplace. The U.S. government generally plays a facilitating role in the economy, but in other markets, firms may find themselves in direct competition with the government or in an industry in which the government plays an active role such as health care, financial services, transportation, manufacturing, agriculture and even food-related products. Governments are not usually seen as the most efficient of competitors but, at the same time, the fact that they also administer the rules of operations—and quite simply their sheer size—can make them a unique competitor.

The country's regional development policies can also have an impact on international operations and the nature of the host market's political environment. Like firms, governments operate with limited resources. How, and where, any given government decides to allocate those resources may increase the likelihood of political threats and risks. Regional development could refer to the government diverting resources to a particular geographic region within the market, or it could mean the allocation of resources to a particular industry, or industries. Frequently these go together, as in the case of technology development and Silicon Valley in California. What any firm must consider beyond just the overall political characteristics of a market is the nuances within that market related to the type of business activities that may be in close proximity to the firm's specific chosen area of operations and both the likelihood and means of government intervention directly affecting its strategies and tactics.

There is also the issue of how the government chooses to administer the market through fiscal and monetary policies. Governments will use a blend of taxes and controls over the money supply to meet their own resource needs and to manage their economy. These fiscal and monetary policies, because they directly affect international businesses, come in the form of taxes, interest rates, exchange controls, and currency rules. Their impact on the firm's ability to obtain capital, and more importantly revenue, is immediate because each of these fiscal and monetary controls is directly related to the cost of capital, the "ownership" of profits (i.e., taxes), and the movement of funds. Economies with a high level of social services will generally have high tax rates—particularly for nondomestic companies. Emerging economies often have more extensive exchange controls (e.g., government-determined exchange rates) and currency rules (e.g., revenue repatriation restrictions). Markets challenged by inflation will use changes in the interest rates to control the value of the local currency. These are just a few examples of what active fiscal and monetary policies can mean to a firm. It is part of understanding the political environment to understand both the role and the nature of these policies—and how they might impact your firm's objectives—in the selected markets of operation.

The aspects of the political environment that can affect international business form the foundation for understanding the nature of the political environment in which the firm has chosen to operate. They generally are the result of the natural, functional government activity within any country. However, there is also the issue of the dynamics of the political environment and the potential for dysfunction in a market. So it is necessary not only to understand the areas in which the political environment can affect operations in an ongoing fashion, but also to take into account the environmental factors that can contribute—often in an irregular way—to political risk.

Environmental Factors Contributing to Political Risk

The catalysts for political risks—the contributing environmental factors—can be individuals, groups or organizations, or simply the result of imperfections within the government and political system. The presence of any of these factors could mean the political environment in the market has a greater potential for creating political threats that would represent significant risks to international firms. Although we discuss this further in the next section, it is important to note when considering these environment factors that political risk is not always the result of firm activities. Your firm may face political threats based on the actions of previous nondomestic firms. It is also possible that your firm has simply been used as a scapegoat for the actions of your home government. The fact that political threats are not always caused by firm activities could be seen, on one hand, in a positive light—that is, your firm didn't do anything wrong. On the other hand, this means that political risk and threats could potentially emerge at any time, which is a compelling reason for any firm, in the course of analyzing the political environment of a market, to consider the existence of these environmental factors.

Because the political environment comprises both government and nongovernment entities, a good place to begin would be those factors, or characteristics, identified with the government side. Firms originating from, or accustomed to operating in, developed markets can find one of the most unsettling characteristics of a market, which can lead directly to political risk, is a lack of democratic institutions. This is not so much an issue of ideology but rather an issue of stability and predictability. From the perspective of business, markets with established democratic institutions have a system in which both the creation and enforcement of laws and regulations is built into a systematic structure. This means a certain amount of objectivity and fairness exists within the political environment in these markets. A lack of democratic institutions can create an atmosphere where laws and regulations are unevenly enforced—to the detriment of international firms—or even nonexistent. The presence of democratic institutions is an indication that there is less uncertainty associated with the political environment in a given market.

The degree to which there are functioning democratic institutions in a market is also related to the existence of potential problem areas in the exercise of authority. Less democratic environments oftentimes have authority exercised through a system in which individuals are appointed to a place of power through a nepotistic, or quasi-nepotistic, arrangement. This leads to unfairness and uncertainty in the way laws and regulations are applied. It can also lead to a scenario in which authority is exercised through threats and coercion, creating a situation in which corruption can thrive. Another potential problem in this type of political environment would be conflict across authority layers and individual power bases. Regardless of how it actually plays out in a given market, a lack of democratic institutions indicates a lack of systematic structure. It can also mean the existence of a power structure in which authority is not based on objective determinants but instead on whom the individuals with authority "know," creating a climate for increased political risk.

On the nongovernment side, there are also factors of which any nondomestic firm should be wary. Any time there are disaffected groups in a society, there is the potential for political instability, which makes international firms an easy target. These disaffected groups—ethnic, religious, and others—generally exist within the current political framework but have concluded that, for whatever reason, their particular cause is not being treated fairly or with enough attention. To make themselves more relevant, they can engage in activities that destabilize the political environment and that, in turn, can mean international firms at best have to deal with increased uncertainty in that market or, at worst, become a target for these groups (e.g., U.S. firms facing vandalism because they are seen as taking away local jobs). At the same time, there may be external threats from groups outside of the political process attempting to gain legitimacy (e.g., terrorists). Although firms can take the stand that these outside groups are simply criminals, they may not be seen in quite that harsh a light by the society—or at least elements of the society—in which they exist. From the perspective of these groups, targeting nondomestic firms makes logical sense in many ways but most specifically because any activities aimed at international companies will both raise awareness of their cause and have less impact in the market than targeting local firms.

Having spent some time considering both the particular aspects of the political environment that can affect international business as well as some of the environmental factors that can lead to political risk, our discussion now turns to the specific nature of political risks and threats. It is certainly vital that, in understanding any market's political environment, a firm have a clear picture not only as to its foundation but also its propensity to produce political problems. However, this process of understanding would be incomplete if there is no consideration put into exactly what kind of threat a firm might be facing and, equally important, what do to about these threats.

Firm-Government Interaction

How Firms and Governments Collide

Understanding the actual nature of political threats begins with understanding the reason, or reasons, behind the threats. There are many ways in which firms and governments interact, but for our purposes in this chapter, we look at only those that represent a threat to an international firm's operations within their chosen host market of operation. Thus, this discussion of how firms and governments interact might be better described as how firms and governments collide. In looking at this collision, we are really looking at the source, or root cause, of political threats. Any political threat that a nondomestic firm faces can be traced back to issues related either to political sovereignty or political conflict. Frequently when a firm faces political threats, whether they be sovereignty or conflict related, they are not the result of the firm violating any specific law or regulation, which means the threats themselves do not represent sanctions as a result of such violations. Instead, the collision of firms and governments—and the threats this collision produces—has more to do with the nature of the firm's operations and the country from which it originates.

A political sovereignty threat is one in which a government sees a firm, its product, or some other aspect of its operations to be a threat to that government's ability to maintain control within its national boundaries— that is, a threat to internal sovereignty. Clearly, it is highly unlikely that your firm, or any other, seeks to supplant a local government. However, the nature of your firm's operations may represent a real problem for the host-market government. Any product that is seen as contrary to the government's social or cultural position will be viewed as a threat (e.g., myriad so-called Western products in markets across the Middle East, Asia, and even Africa where Islam is a dominant political force). Even firms and products that are seen by the host population as being beneficial can represent a threat to the powers that be, as both Google and Yahoo have discovered in China. In the case of these products, what appears to be a better means of accessing and communicating information is seen as a direct challenge to the government as control of information flow is one of the primary means through which the government maintains power. To be viewed as a threat to internal sovereignty, your firm and its product(s) does not have to *intend* to undermine the host government's internal sovereignty; it simply has to be perceived as a threat.

The other cause of political threats to firms would be those that are based on political conflict issues. These may be direct or indirect in nature. Direct political conflict involves conflict between two or more elements of the political environment (i.e., government or nongovernment) where that conflict directly involves your firm's operations, country of origin, or both. Several years ago McDonald's operations in France were the target of attacks—in some cases literal attacks on local McDonald's restaurants—originating from special interest groups (e.g., farmer's unions) because it was viewed as both a threat to French culture in general and local food producers specifically. There was a real demand for McDonald's goods and services in France, as subsequent events have shown, so the company's problems could not be blamed on irresponsibility on the part of the company; rather, what the company did and what it represented as an American firm brought it directly into conflict with parts of the political environment.

Being caught up indirectly into political conflicts can be even more frustrating for a company because these have nothing whatsoever to do with firm operations or products. Such indirect political conflicts have everything to do with the firm's country of origin. In this scenario, the firm—and sometimes its entire industry—becomes a scapegoat in the conflict between governments. Historically the U.S. government has targeted Japanese auto manufacturers in its attempts to open up the agricultural market in Japan to various U.S. imports. The way this works is simple. The U.S. government threatens to place onerous tariffs on Japanese car imports (e.g., 100% of the stated value) if the Japanese government does not open up (e.g., reduce tariffs or other restrictions) their market to U.S. food products. In this situation, there is no question of Japanese firms violating any U.S. laws or regulations nor is there any question as to demand among U.S. consumers for the products. It is simply the most convenient means for the U.S. government to get the attention of its counterparts in

Japan. This is not an isolated example. In late 2011, the Chinese government announced trade restrictions on U.S. cars sold in China in retaliation for U.S. government trade policies toward China and Chinese products. With China the fastest-growing market in the world for U.S. cars, it is not a question of the product being a poor "fit"; it comes down to the fact that U.S. auto manufacturers view China as a means of regaining financial stability and the Chinese government understands the importance of that industry sector to the U.S. economy.

The Results of Firm-Government Collision: Types of Political Threats

The best way to understand the different types of political threats a firm might face is to view these threats from the perspective of how they threaten the firm. The most common types of political threats fall into three basic categories: 1) equity and management threats, 2) earnings and performance threats, and 3) operational threats. Each category of threat has the potential to significantly, and negatively, affect firm operations, but in very different ways. The challenges each represent are unique, and, in some cases, a firm may find it faces threats from more than one category. In any case, the formulation of any plans to deal with political threats requires an understanding how your firm is being targeted—or where the threats will interfere with operations.

Equity and management threats are directed at firm control and management; that is, these types of threats raise the issue of who actually controls your firm's operations in a given host market. Equity and management threats can take the form of direct ownership restrictions with extreme examples being nationalization, confiscation, or expropriation of your firm by the local government. Over the years, this form of threat—governments essentially seizing all, or at least a majority of, a firm's operations—has been associated with developing and emerging markets or those with a high degree of political instability. However, as the marketplace has become more globalized and interdependent, it is less likely that a nondomestic firm will face the loss of its operations in a market. Instead, because governments have discovered both that it is difficult to build an economy when international firms, and the investments they provide, are at risk and that they (governments) are not terribly good at operating at the firm level, other equity and management threats are more likely to represent problems. The most common of these are forced joint ventures and restrictions on home country managers and employees.

In a forced joint venture, the firm is required to cede a majority ownership stake to the local government or one of its representatives. When restrictions are placed on the number of home-country managers and employees who can work in the host-country operations, the firm is forced to hire locally. The logic behind both is simple. The company itself can continue be to run by those with knowledge of the business, but the host-market government retains the ability to control any activities of the company within its borders. Equity and management threats are significant in that your firm loses the ability to maintain sovereignty over itself in the host market, but there may be some slight offset in that although the company no longer has full control over decision making, it is essentially protected from other forms of political threats given that the host government now has a vested interest in the firm's success.

When a firm faces earnings and performance threats, the issue becomes a matter of who profits most from its host-market operations. In an environment marked by earnings and performance threats, the issue is not about control of firm operations but about the flow of revenue and profits obtained by the firm in its operations within the local market. The most common types of earnings and performance threats are some form of exchange control or revenue repatriation restrictions. Exchange controls involve the host government dictating the rate at which monies received in the local market can be taken out of the country. The market exchange rate is ignored in favor of one that will benefit the host economy. Exchange controls can be applied to individual firms, be placed on specific currencies, or, in some cases, involve the government manipulating the value of the currency on a global scale (e.g., the Chinese government's "management" of the value of the yuan). Revenue repatriation restrictions have the same bottom-line effect on firm profits but are applied in a different fashion. Where exchange controls dictate the value of monies that flow out of the market, revenue repatriation restrictions dictate the amount of monies that can be removed from the market. Historically, some Middle Eastern countries have limited the amount of revenue that can be moved out of their markets in any attempt to shore up the value of their local currency by maintaining high levels of so-called hard currency in the market. Whether they come in the form of exchange controls or revenue repatriation restrictions, such threats can significantly hurt the immediate profitability of the firm's host-market operations.

Operational threats are targeted at the means through which the firm operates in the host market. These are not about control or profitability but rather about restricting the means through which the firm can engage in the strategies and tactics for operating in that market. Because operational threats are designed to somehow restrict the means through which a firm interacts with the local market, they are targeted at marketing activities.

Breaking down operational threats along the lines of the four Ps of marketing (i.e., product, place, price, and promotion; see Chapter 2), we can see that it is possible for any—or all—to be affected. A firm's product, and product strategy, can be restricted through the application of product content laws—requirements that the product contain a stipulated amount of local material or labor content. To meet a product content requirement, a firm will likely have to change production processes (which is expensive) and could easily see an adverse effect on product quality. Place, or distribution, could become problematic because the location where a consumer might find the product may be changed or limited. For example, one of the difficulties Japanese beer companies have faced in other markets around the world is the inability to use one of their primary means of distribution—the vending machine. Governments can place parameters on price—ceilings or floors—that inhibit the ability to be competitive and generate revenue. Governments can also limit what can be communicated—and how this communication occurs—which directly affects promotional strategy.

Any, or all, of these three types of political threats demands action on the part of the firm. Even if the firm chooses not to engage in political activities designed to deal with political threats, when faced with such threats, the firm will, at the very least, be required to alter its operations and activities. However, before a response can be formulated, it is advisable to first consider the extent to which your firm is politically vulnerable in its international markets. Not all firms face the same threats in every market around the world. Before the issue of managing political threats is addressed, we must first determine if any political threats actually exist for your firm. This means assessing political vulnerability.

Assessing Political Vulnerability

Assessing political vulnerability is a two-step process that takes into account the fact that political risk and threats can be caused by both sovereignty and conflict issues. In practice, this assessment must address both internal and external issues related to the firm's operational activities in a specific market. The internal, or firm-specific, issues involve the nature of the firm's product(s) and its operational approach to the market. These will change from firm to firm, and the extent to which political threats may be experienced in a given market is only applicable to that firm not generalized to all nondomestic firms operating in that market. The external issues, on the other hand, are market characteristics associated with political risk and threats that can be generalized across nondomestic firms— particularly those from the same home market.

Internal Issues (Firm-Specific)

Several firm-specific characteristics are associated with higher levels of political vulnerability. These can involve the nature of the firm's product, the firm's operational approach to the host market, or simply how the firm and its product offering are viewed by the various players in the political environment. In terms of the product itself, two key indicators of potential political vulnerability are products that have a high service component and those that represent a potential hazard in the marketplace. Service-heavy products tend to be more closely regulated and controlled because of the intangible nature of services and the fact that two of the most lucrative service-sector products are financial management and health care—both of which have the potential to seriously harm individuals as well as the society at large if not properly monitored. Similarly, any product that represents a hazard to individuals or the society is also in a position to face a higher level of political threat. This means not only physical hazards but also social hazards. It takes little imagination to understand that if your product has the potential to physically harm a user, it will be more apt to face higher levels of government regulation. However, many companies fail to consider fully the potential social hazards of their product(s)—something the U.S. market has been especially slow to pick up on compared with other markets around the world. For example, a product such as breakfast cereal marketed to children could be viewed as socially hazardous based on the means through which it is presented (e.g., cartoon characters) and its overall appeal (e.g., candy flavored). The notion that service-oriented products are more likely to face political threats is, perhaps, fairly obvious, but it is incumbent on your firm to consider all possible effects your product might have, or could be perceived to have, on the overall market in which it is placed. As the impact, direct or indirect, of your product increases within a market, so does the potential for political threats.

A second firm-specific area that can lead to increased political threats has to do with your firm's operations in a particular host market. A number of activities on the part of a nondomestic firm can lead to high levels of political vulnerability, but two stand out as being especially problematic. First, whenever a firm is involved in media-related activities, or mass communication, in another market, it is politically vulnerable. As we discussed earlier in the chapter, some firms' products directly involve mass media and information flow (e.g., Google and Yahoo), which makes them immediately vulnerable. However, even a firm with a product that has nothing to do with mass media or information transfer may face similar difficulties if it uses mass communication (e.g., advertising) to market its product.

Any type of involvement in information transfer or the communication of information on the part of the firm—no matter how seemingly harmless it may be—is an indicator of political vulnerability.

The third area that should be assessed relates to how the product is perceived by the various individuals and entities that comprise the political environment. Any time a firm or its product(s) become a point of controversy or debate in the political environment, political threats and risks increase. European manufacturers of the so-called abortion pill saw how this worked in the U.S. market. From their perspective, the pill benefitted society because it enabled the termination of an unwanted pregnancy without the need for an invasive surgical procedure. The individual benefitted by reducing any possible health risk and society benefitted by not having to support unwanted or abandoned infants. At least that was the manufacturer's perspective. Unfortunately, this point of view did not take into account the heated and long-term debate between the pro-life and pro-choice factions in the U.S. political arena. The result was a long delay in the introduction of this type of product because it became a lightning rod in the social debate over the acceptability of abortion in the United States. Anytime your firm, and its product(s), have even the smallest possibility of creating controversy or becoming part of a political debate in a market, you need to be aware that this will more than likely mean political threats and risks.

External Issues (Market-Specific)

Assessing your firm's political vulnerability from the perspective of external issues involves analyzing relevant characteristics of the market rather than your individual firm. Where the internal issues can be very different from one particular firm to another in any given market, the external issues tend to be consistent across firms—especially firms from the same home market. Here we are looking at the nature of the political environment, the interaction between your firm's home and host-market governments and the various administrative procedures that must be addressed to operate in that market.

Starting with the nature of the political environment, one of the primary considerations is the type and stability of the government. As we discussed earlier, the type of government—and how authority is exercised within a nation-state—is an indication of the important players in that market and how the process for creating and enforcing laws and regulations operates. A market in which the type of government is substantially different from the firm's home market can be viewed as threatening in terms of political risk. However, it is also important to take into account the stability of the government. Although a political environment that is different from the home market means learning a new "system" provided that system is reasonably stable (i.e., the political environment is not likely to change significantly), one of the greatest problems associated with political risk—uncertainty—is removed.

There is also the issue of relations between the home- and host-market governments. Poor relations between a firm's home and host market can, as we have discussed earlier, lead to political threats and a higher level of political risk not because of the firm's product or operational activities but simply because it (i.e., the firm) is an easy target. In these circumstances, political threats can be manifest in some reasonably transparent restriction(s) such as a tariff or quota or in some less obvious operational restriction. Lastly, another form of market characteristic that is identified with increased levels of political vulnerability but is easy to overlook as a political threat are the various administrative procedures that must be adhered to when operating in a given market. Even markets with close relations can have levels of bureaucracy that do not match (e.g., customs forms, regulations, procedures). Sifting through the language barriers and investing the time it takes to fulfill these requirements requires resources and can lead to higher levels of uncertainty.

In an ideal world, a firm would select an international market(s) that is stable, had a similar type of government/political system as its home market, and had good relations with its home-market government. Unfortunately, many markets of opportunity do not exhibit these ideal characteristics, and the firm must then determine how best to deal with any political threats. Actively managing political risks can be an involved process, which is why many firms choose to take a passive, reactive approach to any threats originating from the political environment. At the same time, firms that take a more proactive approach to dealing with these threats can frequently gain a unique and significant competitive advantage.

Managing Political Threats

Firms that choose to take a proactive approach to managing political threats have two options. On one hand, they can adopt an internal focus that involves changing or adapting firm operations in the face of a political threat(s). This approach should not be confused with a reactive attitude in which a firm simply adapts to threats originating from the political environment. The internal focus involves assessing any political threat and determining the best long-term solution for the firm—most importantly, one that will create strategic advantage over time. The other approach, an external focus, involves the firm becoming actively involved in a country's political process to manage—and potentially change—the political environment of a host market.

Internal Focus

Adopting an internal focus means that the firm has, to some extent, concluded that the best approach for dealing with the specific political threats they face is through internal operational means. This is not simply a knee-jerk reactive attitude but rather one in which, after careful consideration, the firm has concluded that the issues involved are beyond its scope and ability to proactively manage.

One perspective for dealing with the political environment internally involves the degree to which key operations are either extended toward or pulled back from the host market. Moving operational activities toward the host market (i.e., a "forward" approach) would focus on building political alliances through the business, which would reduce or eliminate any potential threats. For example, seeking joint ventures with local partners would result in sharing of any operational benefits with local partners and, either directly or indirectly, with the local government through additional taxes, jobs, or other means of economic development. Alternatively, the firm may choose a "backward" approach by keeping as many operational activities within its home market. This is somewhat different from exporting as an entry strategy in which the firm desires to maintain product control and/or market immersion. In this situation, the firm would be keeping vital aspects of the firm within a market environment that it understands and over which it has some control. In the present global market, many firms with key proprietary resources, such as technology, attempt, as much as possible, to keep this technology within their home market where they have a better chance of protecting it through its home market's intellectual property laws. In either a forward or backward approach to addressing political threats, the concept is to place the firm in the political environment that is the most advantageous rather than attempting to somehow manipulate the environment.

A third option that is somewhat different from the forward/backward approach, which are essentially "push" strategies given that they involve addressing political threats more or less directly, would be a "pull" strategy. In this scenario, the firm would attempt to increase the dependencies within the host market. The notion is simple: the more dependent a host market is on your firm and its products, the less likely the firm will face political difficulties. Again, this is not about changing the political environment. Instead, it is about changing the perception the market has toward your firm and its product(s). Although some products lend themselves to building dependencies in a market (e.g., petroleum products), others are not so well placed. However, it may be possible to build perceptual dependencies within a market using either an economic approach (i.e., jobs) or a quality-of-life approach (i.e., unique products ranging from pharmaceuticals to safe drinking water). Leveraging the positive aspects of your firm's activities and products becomes a "pull" strategy as the market itself will help to counter any potential threats out of its own best self-interest. This idea of pushing the firm as a good citizen with a positive future impact on the market can be a quick and relatively simple long-term means of reducing political problems in another market.

External Focus

In some cases, a firm may conclude that using the internal focus of dealing with political threats through internal operational approaches is either not sufficient to reduce or remove a political threat or such an approach will not produce a long-term solution. Assuming the firm has sufficient knowledge and resources, it might then turn to an external focus that is targeted at changing the political environment itself. This firm-level political behavior has one of two basic objectives: forestalling (a delaying approach) and absorption (a removal approach). When a firm engages in forestalling, it is using the instability of the political environment to its benefit. For example, if a nondomestic firm seeks to prevent an adverse law or regulation being introduced in the United States, it can engage in political behaviors that can see the piece of legislation is held up in the legislative process (i.e., committees, etc.). Over time, it is conceivable that, unless the proposal has a great deal of political capital attached to it, the potential problem will simply disappear as the powers that be move on to something more visible in the public or political arena. An absorption approach, on the other hand, involves bringing the best interests of the company together with the best interests of an entity, or entities, in the political environment. Regardless of whether an individual firm seeks to accomplish a forestalling or absorption objective the tools available to that firm are essentially the same.

The means through which firms can accomplish their basic political objectives—forestalling or absorption—can be characterized as direct, indirect, or collaborative. It is not our purpose here to develop a comprehensive understanding of each of the approaches. Instead, as part of our developing a deeper understanding of the global business environment—and in the case of this chapter, the political environment—we need to be aware of these tools and how each might function when employed by a firm.

The most common form of direct political activity at the firm level would be lobbying, either domestic or nondomestic. As the names imply, one would be targeted at the home political environment, whereas the other would be focused on the host market. Although over the years lobbying has been the subject of many misconceptions, it is essentially an acceptable professional activity. Just as a firm would hire an attorney to represent its interests in a court of law, a lobbyist is hired to represent the firm's interests in the political realm. Lobbyists specialize in particular areas and have special knowledge of both the players involved as well as the various issues that must be addressed. The question of domestic versus nondomestic simply comes down to the particular threat's point of origin. Another commonly used direct political activity is political contributions. Although in recent years, limits have been placed on the amounts that can be contributed and how those monies can be used—at least in the United States—the nature of elected governments means that resources in the form of contributions will always play a major role in any democratic country around the globe. Inducements—bribes—are frequently mentioned in international business, but the fact is that these are the least attractive form of direct firm-level political behavior. The simple fact is that these "inducements" do not produce any long-term positive change and in many cases are flat-out illegal.

On the indirect side, both public relations and interactions with government agencies—domestic and nondomestic—can also produce constructive results. As is the case with political contributions, public relations are most effective in an environment in which the public has some significant influence on the political environment. Best characterized as a "pull" strategy, using public relations to direct individuals within the political environment can be effective, as shown by the Tea Party movement in the United States. Taking a different tack, enlisting the assistance of government agencies can be both helpful in terms of gathering information (e.g., the *CIA World Book of Facts*) as well as in influencing specific individuals and subcomponents in the overall political landscape.

The third approach, collaborations, are generally considered to be the most effective but have unique potential problems associated with them. A common collaborative firm-level political tool is the political industry alliance. Here, firms of all sizes band together to achieve a specific goal in a specific market. Bringing the resources of a wide range of firms to bear can effect change quickly but at the expense of creating a "level playing field"—one in which no single firm gains competitive advantage. However, by far the most effective firm-level political tool is the creation of "friendships" over time. These relations between the firm and individuals within the political environment are the best means of managing political threats over time but can come at a price—especially when these friendships become centered on individuals rather than the institutions and organizations they represent.

Matching Firm-Level Political Behaviors with Political Threats

So then how are these firm-level political behaviors directed? Matching these behaviors with the political threats that they are designed to "manage" can best be approached by dividing the relevant political threats into three categories. First would be home-market operational restrictions or those laws and regulations directed at firm operational activities that emanate from the home market. Second would be host-market operational restrictions—the same type of laws and regulations but coming from the host market. The third, management performance restrictions, would be those targeted at revenue distribution or firm control, which could originate from either the home or host market.

In the case of home-market operational restrictions, research shows that the most common firm-level political behaviors are lobbying—home and host country, public relations, political industry alliances, and political contributions. Each of these would seem intuitive, particularly for a firm coming from a democratically based political environment, with one exception. Employing host-country lobbying to deal with home-market operational restrictions appears, on the surface, to be somewhat out of place. However, experience shows that when firms commit to a market—a market that has a real, recognized need for the firm's product, particularly when the product in question can significantly contribute to economic development of improving quality of life, such as technology—they can provide sophisticated influence to engage the host-market government in putting pressure on decision makers in the home-country political system.

Turning to host-market operational restrictions, the relevant firm-level political behaviors all seem clear-cut. Firms will go directly to the political environment through lobbying, contributions, or—on occasion—inducements. In an attempt to effect change quickly, they will also band together with other firms in political industry alliances. Similarly, because management and performance restrictions have a swift and immediate impact on profits and revenues, firms will tend to use the two firm-level political behaviors that are associated with the quickest results: lobbying and political industry alliances.

One fact seems inescapable. Although not widely discussed as a part of international business strategy, political behavior, at the firm level, is a tool that many companies use to deal with the uncertainties of the political environment. As we have discussed, this tendency to leave political activities out of any international business strategy discussion may be due to a sense that mixing business with politics smacks of unethical behavior. Alternatively, it may be that these political activities on the part of individual firms may represent a very real means through which to gain competitive advantage causing these companies to be reluctant to reveal their "secrets." Regardless of the reasons, it is fundamentally important when considering the political aspect of the global business environment not only to come to terms with the nature and characteristics of both the home and host market in terms of the relevant laws, regulations, trends, and public opinions that both comprise and influence the political piece of the environment but also to take on board the various tools available to firms—of all sizes—which can be used to manage those potential threats.

Key Legal Issues in International Business

Although, for reasons stated at the outset, this discussion has avoided the legal aspects of the political environment, there are some key issues in the political environment of which firms should be aware. First, there is the growing issue of the interactive nature of individual markets' legal environments. With the increased flow of economic activities across borders, there is always the potential for conflict between laws and regulations. Related to this is the growing recognition of the need for harmonization across markets. The ability to reconcile economies has been the single biggest reason for the success of the European Union but, as recent events have shown, may also be the biggest threat to its survival. In addition, there is a trend worldwide in which international laws and regulations are less focused at the individual level (e.g., price controls) and more on human rights and environmental issues.

Summary

The political and legal environments are two sides of the same coin. For international firms, the legal environment deals with the rules for doing business and the political environment deals with the structures and processes that create those rules. Understanding not only the actual laws and regulations but also the political process through which they are established is vital to anticipate future potential threats and plan for ways of reducing, eliminating, or otherwise managing these threats. This requires knowledge of what constitutes a "nation-state," how political power is exerted, where nondomestic firms can be put at risk and what the resulting risks look like, and finally how to operate proactively within another political environment.

CHAPTER SIX

The Global Competitive Environment: Playing to Win

Introduction

According to former General Electric CEO Jack Welch, "If you don't have a competitive advantage, don't compete." On the surface, this might be construed to suggest that firms either have or do not have competitive advantage. The truth, however, is that every firm—large or small—that has been able to sustain itself in any market has some form of competitive advantage. The difficulty lies in first being cognizant of that advantage, or possibly advantages, and then being aware of how best to leverage them against the competition. In this chapter, we begin by considering the nature of the global competitive environment. From there, we use an established framework—Porter's Five Forces Model—to understand the different forms of competition in the global market, when each represents a competitive threat, and how to deal with those threats. Then we explore how to gain competitive advantage through the process of understanding customers, understanding the firm, and using market information wisely. At the conclusion of the chapter, we develop not only a clear picture of how to assess the competitive environment that a firm might face when it moves outside of its home market but also gain insight into the means through which the firm can not simply survive but also thrive in the face of other competing firms.

The Global Competitive Environment

To understand how the different competitive forces can put pressure on a firm—and by extension how to deal with that pressure—we must first come to terms with the nature of the global competitive environment. The best way to characterize the competitive environment firms face in the global marketplace is *hypercompetitive*. The very nature of the global market with all its complexities (e.g., multiple markets, multiple sources for competitors, market source advantages) means that the competitive dynamic is greatly accelerated. This means that not only is the competitive environment more difficult to understand it also has the potential to change quickly. What then creates this complex and ever-shifting environment?

First, there are the markets themselves. Firms that operate exclusively within their home or domestic market not only have a finite market area in which they operate, they also tend to have a much more limited number of competitors. Although the global market environment may mean that additional firms from other markets may attempt to enter that home market, the reality is that within the confines of its domestic market, the established firm enjoys a reasonably clearly defined set of competing firms that, perhaps just as important, it understands and has experience in dealing with. As the firm moves into the global arena, there are now more markets, each with the potential to change. Often, these markets are also larger than the home market because entering markets with greater growth potential is a key reason for firms to enter into international operations— and as those market opportunities increase, so does the likelihood that competition will as well. There is also the simple fact that more markets of operation means more exposure to competitors of all types—other firms from the home market, firms residing in the host market, and firms from the wide range of other markets in the global economy.

Another feature of this hypercompetitive environment is, as suggested earlier, the nature of the environment itself. The present and future international business environment will be unique—and potentially more problematic—by its complexities as well as the rate and direction in which it has the capacity to change. As we discussed in the opening chapter, the different means through which the various components of the international business environment are configured from one market to another creates complexities, and the firms that are best able to cope with these complexities will have the greatest competitive advantage. This also means the ability to deal with the changes that are inevitable when the marketplace now comprises numerous individual markets. The result is that one requirement for any firm seeking competitive advantage in its international activities is having the flexibility to deal with these complexities and changes because increased scope of operations equals increased risk.

Another aspect of the hypercompetitive international business environment is the fact that many of the traditional tools used to gain competitive advantage are becoming less effective. Businesses traditionally rely on their marketing strategy—as reflected by its use of the four Ps (price, product, place, promotion)—to gain and hold advantage over competing firms. Unfortunately, the changing nature of the global marketplace has altered the nature of these fundamental business tools and made them less universally effective. Advertising, or any mass communication within a market, is no longer simply a matter of using basic media (e.g., television, radio, print). These are increasingly fragmented (e.g., cable and satellite TV) and can be either highly controlled or even unavailable in many markets (e.g., China and India). Pricing is more complicated as markets—and their related currencies—are crossed (witness the ongoing Euro crisis in the European Union). More competitors mean more product choices that make differentiation problematic. Even distribution (aka "place") and having a product in the right place at the right time for customer needs has been transformed by the Internet.

All these factors combined make the international competitive environment hypercompetitive. The number of markets, complex and unstable nature of the business environment as a result of the numerous markets, the attending risk that is attached to this increased scope of business activities, and the fact that the basic tools for competing have changed produces a highly dynamic situation. For any business, to be able to deal successfully with this dynamic competitive environment, there needs to be a level of understanding as to the composition of the competition—who they are, what makes them a threat, and what can be done to deal with that threat(s).

A Framework for the Competitive Environment: Porter's Five Forces Model

Although not strictly directed at international business, this framework is particularly valuable for understanding the global business environment any firm might face for three reasons. First, it recognizes that competition can come in a variety of forms—it is not limited to so-called traditional competitors who sell an essentially similar product. Second, it identifies what might make each of these different competitors, or competitive forces, a threat. Acknowledging that the existence of another firm does not necessarily constitute a threat but rather ascertaining whether a threat actually exists, and why, is an important first step in formulating a strategy for gaining competitive advantage. This leads to the third: the Five Forces Model provides guidance as to the best means of establishing competitive advantage depending on the circumstances. Putting these all together, this framework is a good starting point for a firm trying to get a grasp on the competitive environment in an unfamiliar host market. As the name implies, the model identifies five categories of competition—or *forces*.

Competitive Force 1: New Entrants

A new entrant would be a firm that provides a product, or product line, that is essentially the same as your firm. In other words, the new entrant does not provide a substitute, or alternative, product (to be discussed later) but rather a product that would be viewed by your firm, your established competitors, and the customers in the market as being of the same product and industry "type." In the global marketplace, these new competitors often become especially problematic when they attempt to secure market share in your firm's home market. Alternatively, your firm can easily play this role when it enters a new market. In either situation, the first issue to consider is the extent to which new entrants represent a legitimate threat to existing firms in a given market.

The new entrant becomes a significant competitive force when one of three conditions exists. First, if that new firm is more efficient—that is, it is capable of producing the same quantity and quality of product using fewer resources—it represents a threat. Second, if the product the firm provides is somehow superior that is also problematic. Remember, this so-called superiority is often perceptual (e.g., the notion on the part of consumers that imported goods are better). Third, any new entrant motivated to grab market share can be a substantial competitive threat as the best means of capturing market share (i.e., customers) is a relatively low price.

So if a new entrant demonstrates any of these abilities, what tools are available to the established firms in the market or, from another perspective, what might your firm expect from the existing competitors in a host market? The answer lies in this notion of "new entrant." Clearly the best means of dealing with such a firm is not to plan for how to compete but proactively prevent that firm from entering the market. In other words find a way to increase the barriers to market entry. The traditional means of accomplishing this are either leveraging economies of scale or limiting distribution access. Although larger firms are the ones most readily associated with leveraging economies of scale, this approach can, in fact, be a possibility even for smaller firms depending on the size of the product market—not the overall market.

However, the most common means for effectively keeping a new entrant out is limiting distribution access—and therefore access to customers—through a "blocked" channel. Without access to customers and the revenues they represent, no firm—regardless of their efficiencies, product quality, and reduced price—can successfully enter a market. Therefore, by emphasizing your firm's long-term relationship with distributors and retailers with the implication that adopting an unproven product will jeopardize that revenue stream, it is often quite possible to keep a new entrant out of your home market. Similarly, in assessing a host market, it is absolutely vital for your firm to consider carefully not only the potential product and operational advantages you might have but also your ability to establish and maintain customer relationships in that market.

Competitive Force 2: Suppliers and The Supply Chain

One means of reducing competitive pressure in a host market is to increase the level of assimilation in that market. The logic is clear; by becoming more "local," a firm can begin to enjoy the advantages that come along with being domestic rather than "foreign." To accomplish this means increasing the amount of resources invested as well as the operational activities that are performed in that market. This, in turn, can cause increased dependencies in the firm's host market suppliers and local supply chain. It is easy to forget that, although the supply chain cannot exist without product to move through it, the chain comprises firms that all seek to maximize their revenues.

This creates a somewhat contradictory situation. On the one hand, suppliers and the supply chain need the products in the chain to reach the final consumer successfully and profitably. On the other hand, there is the fact that each member seeks to maximize the revenues it can obtain in performing its tasks in moving the product—which comes at the expense of the other members. In an international market where it is often the case that your firm does not dominate its supply chain, this can present a great deal of competitive pressure.

This pressure becomes a serious problem as soon as the other members of the chain either raise their price or decrease the quality of the tasks and activities they perform. For example, a retailer may demand higher margins either through decreasing the amount they are willing to pay for your product—cutting into your firm's margins—or increasing the price they charge customers—upsetting your product positioning strategy. Or a member of the chain may devote less attention to carefully handling and storing your product, resulting in higher rates of damage and shrinkage.

The best means of dealing with these situations is to identify ways through which the dependency equation is shifted in favor of your firm. Although this may be viewed as difficult in a nondomestic market, it is not impossible if we can understand the various means available for accomplishing such a shift. First, there is the possibility of diversifying within the supply chain. This involves increasing the number of members at each stage—such as diversifying distribution by adding more wholesalers and retailers. Another approach would be to switch to an alternative member to remove the problem, although this can create another set of problems down the road. Some firms find that by combining these two—such as reconfiguring the chain so that it comprises a number of smaller members throughout—can help to reduce or eliminate competitive pressure in the chain but at the added expense of having to manage the increased number of business-to-business interactions. A third approach, used by some firms with sufficient resources, is to "in-source" the required supply chain tasks (e.g., upstream distribution) that can, over time, not only help to alleviate the negative competitive forces but also potentially increase overall firm efficiency.

Competitive Force 3: Customers

It can be difficult to envision customers as being a direct category of competition but considering that their goals are contradictory to a firm's goals they can be seen as a competitive threat. Customers seek to maximize value received and minimize cost incurred. Firms seek to minimize value provided and maximize revenue received. The crux of this competition is the extent to which the firm is willing to establish and maintain a long-term relationship with its customers and, in turn, the customers' recognition that—at least to some extent—one gets what one pays for. In other words, the need to compromise short-term gains in favor of long-term success is the key to dealing with customers as a competitive force. Nowhere is this more true than in an international market. Because a nondomestic firm is often in an inferior competitive position, the need to actively manage the competitive relationship between itself and its customers is vital.

Customers in a host market become a potential competitive threat when they are more demanding than existing customer segments—or have the potential to become more demanding. This change could be the result of other firms and products entering the market or because of a fundamental change (e.g., change in disposable income) in the market. When customers become more demanding, these "demands" generally fall into one of three categories: 1) demands related to better product quality, 2) demands related to better service, and 3) demands related to lower price.

It is not uncommon for nondomestic firms—due to a lack of market knowledge and a lack of confidence—to respond to these demands directly, but this can create a wealth of possible problems because it either legitimizes what amounts to a complaint or criticism of the firm and its product offerings or it puts the firm in an unfavorable revenue position. However, these customer demands are nothing new to any firm. The context (i.e., an international market) has simply changed. To best deal with this category of competitive force, it is useful to consider how this situation would be managed in a domestic market setting.

Most commonly when customers exert competitive pressure by being more demanding successful firms will proactively change customer perceptions. That means not accepting the criticisms but instead raising both customer and market awareness of the value of the product offering. There are numerous examples of this approach. The insurance firm that reminds us that they help "avoid mayhem" is countering customers—and rival firms—who would put premium costs at the top of the list in evaluating the product choices. Or on the other end of the spectrum, the local coffee shop that emphasizes fresh ground coffee to counter the brand awareness and convenience associated with a large franchise. Particularly in an international market where your firm is attempting to establish a long term— and presumably successful—presence, both developing and cultivating a clear and credible positioning strategy, for the product and the firm, is the best means for dealing with customers as a competitive force.

Competitive Force 4: Substitute Products

Although customers can be an easily overlooked competitive force, understanding substitute products in a new market can be the most challenging. In international markets, much of the difficulty associated with these substitute products has to do with identifying what constitutes a substitute in the mind of this new market. In a home, or domestic, market, setting it is not unusual for new entrants and substitute products to be one and the same. However, as your firm is frequently in the position of being new to the host market, the challenge becomes twofold: first, your firm must be able to identify exactly what might be a substitute in this market (i.e., what is your product's "value offering"), and second, as your product becomes more established, how to identify the other firms and products that might be viewed as a substitute in the future.

In an ideal world, your firm would be able to establish its product(s) in a context with few possible substitute alternatives. This means carefully managing perception in the marketplace so that the key elements of your product's competitive advantage are difficult to replicate through the creation of a distinct and credible product positioning strategy. Often nondomestic firms, of all sizes, will choose to build this positioning around some degree of firm-customer relationship—an approach that is both long-term as well as being flexible because it can absorb changes in product, and product line, strategy. Unfortunately, once your firm has a longer presence in that host market, there is always the possibility that other products—new or existing—will be viewed as a viable substitute for your own offering.

In trying to ascertain the extent to which a rival product might be a serious substitute, there are three fundamental characteristics of this competitive force that should be taken into consideration. All else being equal, if there is no significant switching costs to the customer when they make the change from your product to its competitor, these substitutes represent a real threat. There is also the potential that this possible substitute is priced lower. And if the substitute is viewed as providing better performance and/or quality, a problem exists as well. In each of these scenarios, the best means of managing this type of competitive force comes not in a reactive response but in meeting the threat proactively.

Dealing with this competitive force proactively means managing market perceptions. Acknowledging—either directly or indirectly—that a substitute has, for example, performance characteristics that are similar (e.g., Coke Zero vs. Pepsi Max) implies that the competing product is a viable substitute. Rather than ceding this position, the truly proactive firm will change market perceptions as to what constitutes a substitute. This can sometimes be more easily accomplished in a host market given that often nondomestic products—or those seen to be nondomestic—are positioned with some type of image or prestige attached that is difficult to substitute. There is also the potential to leverage limited market knowledge of your firm and its products in establishing a position in the market that cannot be substituted. As was the case with the new entrants, understanding how this competitive force fits into the overall competitive environment is important from the perspective of international operations because a firm could find itself on either side depending on its position in a given market.

Competitive Force 5: "Traditional" Competitors

A traditional competitor is one that provides a product that essentially "looks" the same as your firm's offering. The questions that must be addressed related to this competitive force in a host market focus on the home market—and any associated "source" advantages—along with the characteristics of the market that could create substantial competitive pressure when interacting with these firms. As previously discussed, competing firms may be host-market firms, but they could easily be firms from your home market or originate from another market(s) in the global economy. Based on their market of origin, these firms may enjoy source advantages (e.g., government subsidies, tax breaks, lack of trade barriers) that represent market imperfections (i.e., competitive advantages). Identifying any "source" advantages other firms in the environment might enjoy is the key first step in understanding these traditional competitors.

The second step is to analyze the marketplace in terms of the industry to which these firms belong. In effect, we are looking at the microeconomic environment but from the perspective of the various firms and the competitive conditions in which they operate and interact. The existence of numerous, or equally balanced, competitors means that your firm will need to establish a clear market niche or positioning strategy immediately to deal effectively with these entrenched traditional businesses. Another possible scenario would be a large, but slow-growing, industry in that market. This would call for your firm to assume the role of substitute to reposition the perceptions of the market. There are numerous other potential problematic situations (e.g., high fixed costs, the need to carry a large amount of inventory, a lack of differentiation in the market/industry, high exit barriers) that could also occur. Regardless of the specifics, when the so-called traditional competitors dominate your new market, the best approach is typically to change the perception of the market rather than immediately attempt to take these established firms on at the outset.

Gaining Competitive Advantage

Where Porter's Five Forces Model provides us with a framework for defining the competitive environment in the international business environment along with some basic guidance as to how to best deal with the varying competitive forces, it does not address in any great detail how your firm can prepare to be competitive in a new market(s). To that end, the rest of this chapter focuses on how firms can prepare to gain competitive advantage by better understanding itself—and its products—in the context of a particular market environment. This means understanding your customer(s) in the host market, understanding your firm (and both its capabilities and limitations) in the context of the host market, and also how to take information from that market and use it wisely.

Understanding Your Customers

Any successful business recognizes the importance of understanding its customers. This is much more than just being able to identify them from the rest of the market, or have an idea of their buying patterns.

Understanding your customers means being able to clearly define your product's value from their perspective. It means finding the proper means of wrapping your product, your firm, and everything the firm does into a "package" designed for the customer. And it means understanding how not only to obtain, but to use, information from your customer and, by extension, the market as a whole. Once the firm moves outside of its home market, all of these customer-centered issues come to the fore. Understanding the customer is one of the primary keys to success and, whereas the firm may have had a long track record of interacting with—and understanding—customers in its home market, that knowledge is often critically lacking when the firm enters a new host market. Therefore, it is impossible to understand fully the competitive environment of a host market—and how to gain competitive advantage—without addressing the fact that success within that competitive environment is dictated by the extent to which you, and your firm, can come to terms with its customers.

This understanding of customers in a new host market begins with an understanding of the value your firm and its product(s) bring to those customers. By both understanding this notion of value and then acting on this knowledge, your firm is in a position to create superior customer value in the new market and therefore gain competitive advantage. The "value" that your firm has to offer begins with the capabilities, skills, and resources that your firm possesses *that matter to the customer*. It is all too easy for a firm that excels in a particular market to automatically assume that the same success factors will apply in another market. Brand names that command a premium in one market may be less than desirable—or unknown—in another. Wendy's Old Fashioned Hamburgers is identified with a wholesome young lady is pigtails in the United States, but in the Russian market Wendy's customers prefer scantily dressed young ladies with pigtails—offering free samples (of food, that is).

So understanding your customer begins with the emphasis not just on what your firm does well, but what it does well—in terms of its products—that is interesting and valuable to the customer. This concept then extends beyond the value offering, in the form of the product, to how the firm interacts with its customers. Just as the product offering may be viewed differently by customers in a new host market, so too does the means through which the firm establishes and maintains relationships with those customers, who potentially may vary when compared with the firm's home market. Understanding your firm's product, or value, offering now moves to having a clear picture as to how your firm and its processes, particularly related to service delivery and value creation, can be applied to *do things the way the customer wants*. For example, a small Ohio-based manufacturing firm found competitive advantage in the U.S. market by streamlining order processing—effectively taking the "human factor" out of the equation. As a supplier to the auto industry, the firm proved its ability to provide an endless stream of quality parts to U.S. automakers by anticipating its customers' (i.e., the automakers') needs, yet there was virtually no regular contact between the firm and its customers. This success led the firm to explore other customers in Central and South America, where the firm discovered that the chief draw in those markets for dealing with a smaller manufacturer was the ability to interact directly with the people who made up the organization. In other words, customers south of the border didn't really care about the firm's streamlined efficiencies no matter how important those efficiencies seemed to the firm itself.

Then the firm moves to the actual interaction with the customer—both in real time and from the perspective of establishing and maintaining the firm-customer relationship over time. This means attending to your firm's commitment to its customers, and the service they receive, and then its ability to innovate and change as customers' needs and perception of value evolves. The "real-time" interaction, and the importance of emphasizing a sustained level of commitment to the customer, focuses on what the customer *experiences when dealing with your firm*. A good place to start in a new market when trying to understand the customer experience would be to extend your firm's perspective beyond the value offering and consider what customers experience when there is a disconnect between their expectations and their product experience. How fast and completely are dissatisfaction issues likely to be dealt with, and, based on that process of customer service, what is the likely outcome? It should be obvious that failure to deal with dissatisfaction would be quickly associated with a lack of commitment to your customer. However, managing dissatisfaction properly can sometimes create long-term benefits. When a new, "foreign" firm can quickly and satisfactorily deal with customer problems, it can establish a positive perception of itself in the host market. One of Hyundai's best moves in the United States was to recognize its perceived shortcomings as a Korean car manufacturer and create a long-term, comprehensive warranty policy to customers. When a Hyundai owner has problems with the product, the manufacturer deals with it quickly, turning a perceived weakness into a product strength.

The final piece to understanding your customers, and their perception of value, relates to your firm's ability to maintain a positive relationship with your customers that is difficult for competitors to overcome. This requires the ability on the part of the firm to innovate and change. The goal here is for your firm to continue to get better in the eyes of the customer so that, in the end, they are *not just satisfied, but delighted!* This can come in the form of product improvements or improvements in the service interaction. Sometimes it can even be in the form of product associations, such as those created in advertising. Whatever form this "delight" takes, it is the result of the firm working not just to ensure the customer is "satisfied" (i.e., essentially neutral in their product reactions over time) but in an active mind-set focused on the positive feelings and experiences associated with buying and using your product. Car manufacturers from around the world have figured this out, as evidenced by the emphasis placed on cabin features and ergonomically designed interiors. Enjoying the act of driving—or interacting with the car—is an area in which customers from all cultures can be "delighted." Anytime your firm, and its product, can *exceed* customer expectations it places itself in a position to have a long-term relationship with its customer base.

Customer Perception Is Reality

It is not uncommon, especially when a firm is new to a market, to lose sight of the influence customer perceptions regarding your firm and its products have on gaining competitive advantage. As we saw in the previous discussion of understanding customer value, your product is much more than the bundle of values it represents. This means that what customers think or believe is what they act on, which makes those perceptions reality. When a firm enters a new host market it naturally will focus on understanding its product, but that interpretation can be clouded by the firm's view of its product offering(s) as well as previous experience dealing with customers from other markets. Obviously that knowledge is not to be discarded, but it must be placed into the context of the new customers and focused through the lens of their reality. For example, a small Midwestern software firm specializing in data search tools discovered that, although it believed the speed of the search was a crucial feature, customers in Mexico perceived that too fast a search would yield incomplete results. In the end, the firm slowed down the product to accommodate this perception in the Mexican market.

In understanding the connection between your new customers and your product, it is always a good starting place to remember that different customers buy different kinds of value. Some focus on the product itself, others on the interaction with the firm and the process of obtaining the product, and others seek out what the product represents. Keeping this in mind, there are four basic categories of product "values" that customers in any market can view as important when selecting your product over a competitor's product. These "values" that customers seek encompass all the facets of a product. It is unusual—perhaps unheard of—for any one firm to provide a product that excels at all of these values. At the same time, a firm that has a clear understanding of the multifaceted nature of product value is the one most likely to enjoy the highest level of success, whereas firms that take a narrower view of product value are frequently handicapped in the competitive environment. Having an expanded perspective when it comes to the various characteristics customers seek from a product provides a firm with more tools in which to gain competitive advantage. Outside of the firm's home market, this understanding becomes even more important as customers in different markets may place emphasis on different aspects of the product's "value bundle" (i.e., the different aspects of value).

The first of these "values" is product value. This relates primarily to the functionality of the product in the mind of the customer. Product value is how well the product performs—or is perceived to perform. This product value is often considered to be synonymous with product "quality," but the notion of quality can be difficult to understand, especially in the context of consumers in a market where your firm has little, or no, knowledge. The notion of quality is somewhat nebulous and can apply to all facets of a product. For example, a product might be a "quality" item if it performs a single task well (e.g., Chicago Cutlery), if it performs that task well over time and is considered reliable (e.g., John Deere tractors and lawn mowers), or if it has a respected brand name (e.g., Mercedes-Benz automobiles).

Because this concept of product quality is difficult to define, to focus your firm's customer strategy in a new host market, it is best to concentrate instead on product quality in terms of product functionality. That is, what will the customers use your product for, and how well will it perform that function(s)? It may sound superficial, but keep in mind that what one group of customers uses your product for may be very different from customers in another market. The firm that sold spray attachments for garden hoses designed for washing cars in the United States could have easily ignored some Asian and European markets based on the car-washing behavior of consumers in those markets. Instead, the firm discovered that the product could be popular for cleaning homes, landscaping, and a variety of other outdoor uses. Gaining customer advantage in a host market requires your firm have a well-developed understanding of this notion of product value—and this begins with answering the following questions: "What will the customers in this market use our product for?" and "How well will it perform that particular function(s)?"

The second "value" is service value. This is related to product value in that it is also associated with product functionality, but from a different perspective. Where product value applies to how well the product performs its functions each time it is used, service value relates to how well the product will perform over time. Thus, service value has two main aspects to consider. On one hand, service value is associated specifically with product reliability. However, it is also associated with the recourse available to the customer if the product fails to perform. This is where firms can use the multifaceted perspective of value to begin gaining competitive advantage even if their product is not necessarily the best in terms of initial performance. It is quite conceivable that your firm's product is not the market leader in terms of that initial performance or in performing the task for which it is purchased. However, if it can perform that task(s) at a reasonably acceptable level consistently over time, customers in that market could easily view it as superior. This strategy has been used effectively to gain competitive advantage in host markets by firms with high involvement consumer goods (e.g., Hyundai and its comprehensive 10 year/100,000 mile warranty) to lower involvement, even routine purchases (e.g., Walmart's liberal return policy). In the case of both of these companies, and the numerous other firms that have also adopted this approach, they know that their products are not superior from the perspective of product value but that they perform at a reasonably high standard that—if it can be sustained—will provide a high enough level of customer satisfaction, resulting in competitive advantage. Perhaps your firm and its products are not perceived to have the highest level of product value in a market, or because of lack of familiarity, the customers in a host market do not have a clear picture of the level of product value to expect from your offering. Leveraging service value can help to overcome any problems—real or perceived—your firm might encounter in a new market.

The third value that customers might associate with your product offering is personnel value. While in the U.S. market, this may be the least emphasized of the four product "values," it still has a relevant place in the American market and could be argued to have more significant spot in other markets. Personnel value is that which is obtained through interaction not with the product offering but with the firm and its representatives. When a person says, "one of the big factors in my purchase was the salesperson's knowledge of the product," he or she is acknowledging the importance of personnel value. In markets with a high cultural emphasis on social interactions, personnel value can be a critically important piece to emphasize in the value bundle that is your product. Anytime your firm, through interactions with customers, can enhance the perception of its product offering, it not only improves the overall perception of the product, it also lays the foundation for an ongoing relationship with customers. This is especially critical when your product offering has a substantial service component and/or your firm operates in a business-to-business market—both of which tend to be unique in that the firm's representative in many cases becomes the personification of the product offering.

The last of the value components—image value—is influenced the most by customer perception rather than objective inputs. In a materially based culture such as the United States, most people understand the concept of image value—to a large extent, it is synonymous with brand equity. Image value is, simply stated, the value attached to possessing the product offering. The notion a particular brand is "better" than another is a basic fact in marketing. Indeed, there is often little connection between product value (i.e., functionality) and image value (brand name). There was a period of time when Mercedes-Benz automobiles were listed among some of the least reliable cars being sold in America; however, these cars still commanded a premium price solely because of their image. As markets have become increasingly globalized, branding and brand strategy have come to the forefront for virtually all companies. If your firm has a strong brand presence in a new market, possesses the expertise to develop such an image, or has a brand that lends itself to creating a strong image, this particular facet of value should not be overlooked.

Teasing out the complexities of the values associated with your total product offering—and how that value configuration may change from market to market—requires time and resources, but it also gives your firm a much wider view of product strategy with an accompanying increase in tools for gaining competitive advantage. From this standpoint alone, developing a clear picture of the complex nature of the product offering based on these different values would seem to be a must for firms operating outside of their home market. However, there is another compelling reason for any firm to have this deeper understanding of its product offering within the context of each market in which it operates. The reason, simply put, is this: things change and values migrate.

In the case of even the most established products, changes in the market environment can significantly change the nature of the product and the values customers seek from that product. Sony's PlayStation game consoles have, in their various incarnations, recognized the changing nature of its product value. Where the first generation was all about high-resolution graphics and other game-oriented features, by the third generation, it was much more than the core gaming features and now could be used as a web browser that, among other things enabled it to be used to stream movies à la Netflix, play both DVD and Blu-ray format movies, and offered a free online gaming function. In short, Sony understood that the product value and functionality definition had moved well beyond just individually loaded games. A myriad of similar examples exist across all the different value classifications: increases in service value can change negative country-of-origin effects. The convenience of online trading has meant a decline in emphasis on personnel value and an increase in product value in the financial services world. Increased exposure on the part of consumers to goods from China, India, and other newly rising economies has changed perceptions of product along with a shift in the image value associated with product from those markets.

The firms that have obtained, and sustained, competitive advantage in multiple markets around the globe actively monitor and manage shifts in the market environments to anticipate and accommodate these changes in what constitutes "value." Among the most proactive firms, this means not just reactively responding to shifts in value patterns but anticipating and managing those shifts by embracing a basic notion: "value alone is not enough; delight lasts." As part of a product strategy, this can be approached in several ways, but the most effective when dealing with multiple customer segments spread over more than one market involve either "amplifying" existing values or redefining those existing values. In some cases, firms have been able to take aspects that appeal to customers in one market and apply those to another. For example, Frito-Lay learned—via its Walker's Chips brand—that snack buyers in the United Kingdom expect seasonal flavor varieties. In the summer months, this means Chinese BBQ rib flavor, and over the Christmas holidays, turkey and gravy along with lamb and mint jelly flavors. Giving this concept a market-based twist, the company's Doritos brand has remained strong in the United States with its strategy of providing limited-time flavors (e.g., Late Night Cheeseburger) and mixing flavors (e.g., cool ranch and buffalo chicken wings). The result: "delight" on the part of customers based on the fact that the company is going beyond the established value parameters and presenting new values the customer hadn't originally sought—but now finds attractive. Gaining superior competitive advantage means this twofold understanding of your customers' sought for value bundle and a proactive approach to meeting and exceeding those expectations. This then raises the question, how can a firm establish and maintain the market connections necessary to make this work, especially in a nondomestic market setting? This answer is: listen to your customer.

Listening to Your Customer

The process of listening to your customer is particularly crucial in an unfamiliar market. When a firm enters a new market, it is often all too easy to fall into the trap of viewing your product offering in terms of product category—which, in turn, results in a view of the product's value configuration based on home-market customers. As we have established, one of the key distinguishing features of the international market environment is the fact that customers in another market may have a very different perspective of a product—what it offers, how it is distinct, and how it might be used—than your current customer base. Therefore, developing a framework for tapping into their thoughts related to your firm and its product is essential for gaining competitive advantage.

A good place to begin in this process is to allow your customers—current and potential—to describe their product experience through a "storytelling"-type format. Using a focus group format built around questions related to product use and context can create a deeper understanding of not only how the product is used but also the underlying value configuration different groups of customers may seek. Being able to hear firsthand, in an interactive format, from customers about your product can go well beyond other forms of market research such as surveys that, although seemingly more cost-effective, do not always provide clear insight into the complexities of customer thinking.

Kimberly-Clark's experience with its pull-up diaper product in England provides an excellent example of how allowing your customers to tell their "story" can provide invaluable direction in formulating a successful product strategy. The difficulty with disposable diapers as a product is that there is a fairly small window in which to sell the product: most children will at some point progress beyond the product (typically within 24 months). The executives at Kimberly-Clark found the British market to be uniquely attractive because children in this market tended to wear disposable diapers longer than in other markets in which the product was marketed—most notably, the United States. They company concluded that parents in the United Kingdom, for whatever reason, liked the product concept better than parents in the States and so initiated a marketing research program to try to ascertain why these customers liked the product so much, hoping to be able to use the information to prolong usage in the United States. Allowing their customers to engage in storytelling quickly revealed that rather than having an affinity for disposable diapers, British parents had a high level of antipathy for the product.

The crux of the matter was that parents viewed the movement away from diapers to be an important point of child development. At the same time, lifestyle concerns—most notably a relatively high incidence of children being in full-time child-care program—made it difficult for parents to be able to create the structure necessary for their kids to become "potty trained" at a young age. Taking this into account, Kimberly-Clark approached the problem from the perspective of addressing the stigma, on the part of parents, attached to their product. The result was the "pull-up," a combination of disposable diaper and underwear. Through a positioning strategy targeted at the association of the product with the development of children who wore the product (i.e., "I'm a big girl/boy now"), the stigma was removed. Parents were now much more positive in their attitude toward the use of disposable diapers—given the new product form—and actually more likely to use the product over a longer period of time. In the end, this increased revenue stream was achieved because the firm was able to contextualize its understanding of its product offering through direct interaction with its customers.

Being able to engage your customer through these kinds of direct interaction provides invaluable insight as your firm tries to fully understand customers in a new market. Storytelling, or meeting them as part of a service value strategy, can give valuable clues as to how your product might be used, what configuration of values these customers seek, and what other products might be considered to be competitors. However, these activities presume your firm has a group of customers in that market that you can access—crossing cultural and language barriers. An alternative activity that requires much fewer resources is to observe customers—yours and your competitors'. Watching your customers—current and potential—does not tell you *why* they may behave in a certain manner like a direct interaction might, but it will help to tell you *what* they will do under certain circumstances. This can help to build an understanding of customer patterns and can also overcome cultural and language barriers.

Watching and talking with consumers forms the foundation for understanding customers in a new market. However, there is one additional piece of this process that cannot be overlooked: dissatisfied customers. In attempting to understand your customers, especially those vital new customers who take the risk on your firm and product when you enter a host market, it is impossible to overstate the importance of understanding why some are dissatisfied. When customers are dissatisfied, they buy less, buy less frequently, or can easily move to a competing product. Furthermore, when customers are dissatisfied, your firm is often the last to know. Past research has shown that although only about 5 percent of dissatisfied customers actually complain, for every complaint, upward of two dozen customers may actually be dissatisfied, with perhaps a quarter of those with serious and legitimate complaints. In short, dissatisfied customers may represent only the tip of the proverbial iceberg of problems, something no firm new to a market can afford to alienate. However, these dissatisfied customers can be used to some advantage over time. Successful firms know that the cost of complaint resolution is often less than 25 percent of the cost of attracting a new customer and that resolving complaints in a satisfactory manner can create loyal customers.

Understanding Your Firm

Having a good understanding of your host market customer is essential for success, but it is not sufficient. Your firm also needs to have a clear idea of what it can realistically expect to accomplish—and what that means for connecting with these new customers. In other words, your firm needs to come to terms with its capabilities and then develop a basis for differentiating itself from the competition.

As we discussed earlier, it is important for any firm to be able to establish the things it does well that matter to the customer. However, this does not presume that a firm can be all things to all customers. In establishing firm capabilities that can be leveraged in a new market, it is best to take a two-sided perspective. First, your firm must establish its core capabilities; that is, what is it fundamentally good at? Black & Decker sees its core capability as designing and manufacturing small electrical motors. Citicorp considers its core competency to be systems management. Technology Concepts Inc. (a small—less than 20 employees—Midwestern software developer) knows it excels in user interfaces. Understanding core competency is not about short-term successes; it is about the essence of the firm that, in turn, becomes the foundation for products that resonate with customers and ultimately create competitive advantage.

At the same time, there is the other side of this perspective that also needs to be addressed: what is your firm's differentiating capabilities? Core capabilities—what your firm is good at—must be determined. But it should be implicit that any identified core capabilities should be capabilities that can be leveraged to create competitive advantage. In other words, truly understanding your firm in the context of a new market—from the perspective of customers in that market—means not losing track of what made your firm successful in its established markets in the first place. Only then can your firm begin to understand its competitive strengths and weaknesses in a new host market.

From there, your firm must then decide how it intends to create this competitive differentiation. Obviously one approach to gaining competitive differentiation is through product leadership. Products that are viewed as new to a market are frequently associated with innovation and competitive superiority. This could be real, objective product superiority, or it could simply be based on customer perception—and perhaps lack of knowledge—in a new host market. U.S. import car buyers consistently viewed Jaguar automobiles as high-end luxury products—and therefore superior to domestic alternatives. The truth was that based on both features and reliability, over the years Jaguars were nothing special. However, if the market believes your product to be superior in some way, even perceptually, your firm may be in a position to gain competitive differentiation through product leadership—in the case of Jaguar, a luxury product positioning strategy.

But what if your product isn't superior? Another approach involves operational excellence in which your firm focuses on delivering an overall "product package" rather than superiority in a more narrow sense (e.g., product quality). For example, delivering a sufficient—but not superior—level of product quality, price value, and ease of purchase (e.g., Walmart) may mean not only does your firm not have to worry about not having the best product on the market, it may gain its competitive advantage by having the best overall product bundle when compared to other firms. As we discussed earlier in the chapter, what the customer seeks from your firm can be much more than just a tangible product—the other values of time, energy, and image also can play a significant part in gaining competitive advantage, and these hold real hope for firms that have, or are perceived to have, a product that in and of itself does not compare well with the competition.

So on one end of the spectrum, we have firms that seek competitive differentiation through product leadership. Then, in the middle, we have the firms that seek to win with a balanced product bundle. Last, on the other end of the spectrum, we have firms that seek to gain competitive advantage through customer intimacy. Frequently referred to as "mass customization," this approach to competitive differentiation is built around projecting on to your customer a feeling that your product—indeed, your company's entire approach to the marketplace—is built around his or her own individual needs. This concept of "taking care of all your needs" can be particularly successful in a host market where familiarity and awareness of your firm and its products may be low. As an "outsider," any time a company can build a standard of customer care into its strategy, it has the potential to garner higher levels of competitive differentiation. The simple fact is that there are not many customers around the globe who see higher levels of a corporate focus on their particular needs and wants as a bad thing.

Using Market Knowledge Effectively

All of the discussion in this chapter presumes your firm has a sufficient level of market, customer, and competitor knowledge. That being said, it would be advisable to consider some of the mistakes to avoid if your firm is going to use this knowledge effectively. One of the most common mistakes is falling into the trap of gathering more information before making a decision. It is easy to say, "We need more information to make an informed decision," but the truth of the matter is that no firm ever has complete and comprehensive data—on anything. Instead, this mistake is probably more closely associated with the statement, "We are afraid of the unknown." Failure to act will lead to failure, period.

A second error is the notion that getting information faster means better information. Although it is always best to have up-to-date, accurate marketing information, speedy data collection for its own sake can lead to superficial information. Timeliness means having a clear understanding on what information is being gathered and why that, in turn, suggests a certain level of deliberateness exists in the process.

The third mistake to avoid would be falling into the trap that your firm intuitively knows what information is important to gather at the outset. Different markets—and their distinct customer and competitive environment—potentially have an entirely different set of relevant issues. Understanding this new competitive environment means it cannot be assumed that what is important in one market automatically applies to another.

Fourth, and finally, firms can also erroneously make the assumption that they know how to analyze and apply information effectively. Too often this means trying to create empirical, objective analyses from qualitative, subjective data. Putting subjective information into an objective format for the sake of "clean" analysis can mean losing much of the information's value. In a new market, the value of this qualitative information cannot be overstated because it can provide a deep insight into the market's complexities (e.g., customer product perceptions) even though it is harder to associate with specific answers. In the end, market information is necessary for successfully navigating the competitive environment of a new market, but every firm needs to recognize its purpose; that is, market information is supposed to provide informed input on which strategic decisions can be made; it is not about removing all uncertainty.

Summary

As I established at the beginning of the chapter, being competitive is as much—if not more—about understanding your firm and its products as it is understanding your competition. Many firms have a distinct competitive advantage, or the means to gain a competitive upper hand, but lack the vision to achieve this goal in an international context. In this chapter, we focused on the three areas that any firm must address both to understand the competitive environment and, by extension, to achieve competitive advantage in a nondomestic setting. This means: 1) understanding the nature of the international competitive environment, 2) identifying the firm's primary type of international competitor(s) and how best to deal with them, and 3) the strategies and tactics for not only gaining but also maintaining competitive advantage in a new market.

The Firm's Impact on the Environment and Future Trends

Introduction

Throughout this book, we have operated under the assumption that the impact different elements of the international business environment may have on a firm would affect its ability to operate and, ultimately, succeed in its international endeavors. Our approach has been that a host-market environment has the potential to detrimentally affect firm operations and performance. This means that to meet any threats, the firm needs to be prepared and, wherever possible, proactively manage those threats. However, to have a complete understanding of the international business environment, we must also consider an alternative perspective. That is, to what extent does the firm's operations in, and interaction with, a host market have an impact on that market's environment? By carefully considering any possible impact—positive or negative—firm operations might have on a given market, we will be in a better position to plan for the results and, perhaps, leverage positive influences to create a more favorable environment in that market.

Placed into an overall, or macro, context (i.e., beyond consumers, suppliers, and competitors), a firm can have an impact on a host-market environment in three broad areas: economic, political, and social-cultural. Just as any given aspect of the host-market environment may work either for or against a firm's ability to meet its objectives, the firm's impact on the host market in these three areas can be positive or negative. From an economic perspective, a firm may provide jobs or contribute to currency instability. It may help to increase trade between the host and home market or contribute to political instability in the host market. The firm may provide products that local consumers demand or change consumption patterns. Just as the market environment puts pressure on businesses, individual firms, through participation in that market, can help to shape the market environment. To fully use this to the benefit of the firm, the best starting place is not with minimizing negative aspects but rather to identify the positive impact(s) the firm has on the host market that can be leveraged.

The Positive Impact of "Foreign" Firms

There are several ways in which a firm can have a positive impact on its host market, and these are not limited to big ticket investment. Too often the assumption is that firms can only have a positive impact through large financial commitments such as engaging in direct investment that, in turn, contributes jobs—directly and indirectly—to the host economy. Although such investment would clearly benefit the host market, that level of expenditure is beyond the means of most companies. Financial investment does not have to be viewed solely in terms of the amount of investment. Furthermore, there are other ways in which a firm can leverage the benefits associated with its operations.

Financial Investment in the Host Market

Perhaps the firm does not have the financial resources to create jobs or directly facilitate significant economic change in the host market. This does not mean that there are no benefits accrued to the host market from other smaller investments a firm might make. One area that is frequently overlooked, especially by American companies, is the value of the links with "outside" firms to the host-market firms. The financial investment required to operate in a new market means increased interaction with local firms, which provides a basis for information flow and the potential for future opportunities for both sides. Financial investment in the host market can also result in increased productivity in that market as more resources are made available both directly and indirectly. Alternatively, host market companies may enjoy improved efficiencies as the result of learning better process implementation from the outside firm. Clearly, being able to facilitate capital formation and provide a financial base for economic development has the potential to provide a real, positive impact in a host market, but other more affordable forms of financial investment are also valuable to that market.

Trade Advantages for the Host Market

Another area of positive impact might be the increased trade advantages for the host market that are the direct result of firm activities in that market. These can come in the form of expanded export opportunities or in the increased availability of imported products. It is easy for companies, particularly U.S. companies, to forget the real opportunity being able to operate in its home (i.e., U.S.) market represents. For all the talk of recession and economic hardship, the U.S. market remains one of the most stable and lucrative in the world. Firms that operate in host markets are often seen by businesses in that market as a means to enter the other firm's home market (i.e., U.S. firms can be seen as a potential aid for entering the U.S. market). This should not be discounted and, as a positive influence, is available to firms of virtually any size. Alternatively, an outside firm may be viewed as providing trade advantages to a host market through an increased availability of products in that market. This would be reflected in an increase in the quality of life through lower prices, wider product selection, new products, or better products. By increasing trade between the home and host market, firms of any size may, simply by virtue of their international operations and excluding investment in the host market, have a positive impact.

Technological Improvements in the Host Market

A third area in which an individual company can be seen to have a positive influence on a host market would be through technological improvements. One way to look at this would be through the impact of research and development activities. By introducing technological improvements in a market, the level of sophistication (e.g., application, or use, of technology) in that market goes up—with the accompanying increases in productivity and efficiency. Technological improvements may also take the form of industrial upgrades, which can increase production quality, making local products more competitive. Or technological improvements may be in the form of new capital equipment, which improves the market's potential for sustained economic growth. In either case, like the trade advantages discussed earlier, these positive technological improvements could be provided by businesses of all sizes and resource bases.

Labor Improvements in the Host Market

A common area often identified with nondomestic firms having a positive impact on a host market is through the provision of labor improvements. However, like financial investments in a host market, too often this is viewed solely in terms of providing a significant number of jobs. Obviously, whenever a single firm can make a difference by adding jobs or otherwise increasing labor resource utilization in another market, that represents a positive impact. Unfortunately, such a narrow view of labor improvements is only open to large firms. For other firms, leveraging labor improvements means expanding the definition of "improvements" beyond simply providing jobs.

One simple approach is to contextualize labor improvements as a four-step progression. The first step is providing employment. From there, the second step would be to provide training targeted at improving employees' occupational skill set (i.e., enable them to "specialize" in a particular task or set of skills). The third step—learning effects—moves beyond occupational skills to those that have a broader application (e.g., reading, mathematics, computer/technology) that could be used in a variety of employment settings. The fourth, managerial skills, represents those that increase organizational and operational efforts through improved higher-level decision making. As the labor improvements progress beyond the first step, the impact on individuals is significantly greater, and because these improvements in the labor pool are not solely number-focused, the positive impact on the host market can be achieved by firms of all sizes.

General Improvements in the Host Market

In addition to those discussed above, there are several other ways an individual firm can leverage its operations within a host market in a positive fashion. For example, firms coming from developed markets are often in a position to provide insights into "clean" production techniques. A low impact on the environment is often a legal requirement for companies manufacturing in these developed markets. Having already found a way to be efficient while maintaining that low environmental impact could easily represent a benefit to less developed markets where "dirty" production techniques are the norm. A related area would be improved by-product disposal. A common problem area for many markets around the world is pollution resulting from increased economic activity. Introducing disposal methods that cut down on this pollution clearly represents a benefit to the host market. A third general improvement would be the consistency that comes along with the introduction of company-wide standards. These improve production efficiency and control as well as overall product quality when the product hits the market.

Any, or potentially all, of these areas discussed could be available for small, medium, or large firms to use in making the case for being a good citizen in any given host market. At the same time, it is important to recognize that not all markets have the same potential for achieving these positive benefits. That leaves us with the following question: what type, or types, of host markets have conditions best suited for the leveraging of these operational areas of positive impact?

Host Market Conditions Best Suited for Making a Positive Impact

There are several types of markets where a firm, of any size, has a greater chance to make a visible positive impact. That is not to say that these particular market conditions should be a major component of the market selection process. Rather, by identifying the opportunity to leverage firm activities in certain kinds of markets, a firm will be in a better position to maximize the positive results of its operations in those markets.

Perhaps the host market most obviously well suited for making a positive impact would be a lesser developed country (LDC). We discussed in previous chapters that LDCs can represent significant opportunities for firms with products that can contribute to the market's development (e.g., construction-related products). Given that a lesser-developed host market is likely lacking in any substantive domestic investment funds, any operational activity from outside firms is likely to have a positive impact. For those firms that have targeted an LDC, either as an operational location or as a source of revenue generation, there should be a conscious awareness of the positive aspects of its local activities, and those should be leveraged wherever possible.

Another type of host market where a firm might leverage its activities in a positive way would be one in which there is limited product sophistication or availability. This would be closely tied to the quality-of-life discussion related to demand and the economic environment. Providing new products, a wider range of product choices, or improved product quality standards are all potentially positive aspects of firm operations. Virtually any product that is viewed as fulfilling latent demand or providing for unanticipated value could be viewed as contributing to improved quality of life in the host market. Such products might range from over-the-counter pharmaceuticals or sophisticated technology right down to simply providing good quality, affordable consumer products such as food, clothing, or building materials. Too often firms, many of which have products in the mature stage of the product life cycle in their home market, take for granted the contributions their products can make in terms of an improved lifestyle for consumers in a host market.

Related to this notion of improvements to the host market through increasing product availability and sophistication would be the ability of outside firms to aid in addressing the issue of limited resource access. Any market seeking to achieve higher levels of development, yet lacking the necessary resources, will view outside firms in a positive light. If the firm is directly involved in providing capital and other forms of financial resources, improvements to the labor force, or even access to external markets, these should be proactively used to the benefit of the firm in that host market.

A final area of positive impact would be in the firm's operational philosophy. Many times in a host market, the perception of nondomestic firms is one of exploitation. Whether this is based on the treatment of local workers, the movement of revenue outside of the market, or just the overall perceived attitude of the outside firm, there is always the possibility of the firm being viewed as a less than responsible player in the host market. Adopting a more proactive approach to resource transfer benefits (i.e., promoting the positive aspects of firm operations) and consciously avoiding activities that could be viewed as exploitive will assist the firm in developing a local persona that facilitates rather than hinders its ability to achieve its objectives in that host market. This then leads to the issue of negative consequences of firm operations in a host market—that is, what are the criticisms a firm might face in a host market, and what are the best ways of dealing with these criticisms?

The Negative Impact of "Foreign" Firms: Common Criticisms

There are several common criticisms a firm might encounter related to its international operations and its impact on a host market. Understanding the extent to which these may present a substantial problem for the firm means both identifying those criticisms that the firm may, or may not, encounter as well as how to address each proactively.

One area in which these criticisms can present themselves involves the impact of the firm's operations. Specifically, there is the issue of the firm engaging in resource or technology transfer that is too expensive, too closely controlled, or too limited. There may be no intent on the part of the firm to operate in a negative fashion; these issues may simply be a by-product of the firm's approach to a given market. Similarly, firms can be criticized for perpetuating a host country's dependencies through an emphasis on centralized control originating from the firm's home market. For example, it has been estimated that of the 100 largest multinational corporations in the world, fewer than 20 have a majority of their assets outside their home market. As is the case with resource or technology transfer, this may be the result of the firm's operational approach rather than any intention to exploit the host market. In either case, firms that encounter problems with these criticisms generally have failed to take into account the fact that they are often under more scrutiny in a nondomestic setting. Active use of public relations to leverage positive aspects of the firm's operations in the market (as discussed earlier) is the single best way to prevent these criticisms from getting out of hand.

Another area where firms can encounter criticism relates to what could be viewed as exploiting the host market. An area of possible exploitive activity on the part of the firm would be the sale of "unnecessary" products. Firms coming from markets where branding becomes a key part of the marketing strategy can easily overlook the fact that markets without that same level of familiarity with the branding concept (in particular premium brands) could conclude that those products are unnecessary. However, it is important to consider who—or perhaps more importantly, who is not— leveling these criticisms. It is unlikely that the firm's customers will be at the heart of these complaints. Instead, competitors or even other outside influences (e.g., elements of the political environment) are more likely the source. Here it is important first to identify the source of the criticism so that an appropriate course of action can be developed (e.g., dealing with competitors requires a much different approach than dealing with elements of the political environment). It may be that after careful consideration, the conclusion is that these do not represent a significant overall threat, that the source of the threat is irrelevant, or that openly addressing the threat simply serves to legitimize the argument against the firm's product.

There may also be the claim that any given firm exploits the human capital in the host market. Frequently this relates to the firm's "exploita-tion" of local labor, but it can also refer to the perception that the firm reserves its best jobs and employment opportunities for home-country employees. In the case of the former, these complaints often originate not in the host market but in the company's home market. For example, manufacturing workers (and their unions) in the United States would argue that paying employees in Asia a fraction of the U.S. workers wage is exploitation. The reality may be that the host market equivalent of, say, $5 per hour, although significantly less than the U.S. employee would expect, represents a significantly higher wage than these local workers could expect from another job or employer. That being the case, it may be best to simply ignore the criticism. Regardless, knowing the origin of the problem is essential to determining not only how, but whether, to address the situation. As for reserving the best jobs for home-country employees, there may be a sound operational reason for doing so, in which case the best course of action would be to deflect the complaint by emphasizing other positive aspects of firm operations in that market.

At the end of the day it is always important for the international firm to be able to contextualize itself in its international environment. Assessing the various aspects of the international business environment is essential to identify areas of threats and how to proactively manage these as well as areas of opportunities that may be the natural result of differences between the home market and various potential host markets. This means being able to go beyond simply an analysis of the international business environment and being able to understand how the firm might interact—positively and negatively—with the environment in which it has chosen to operate. For the firm to be able to achieve this level of understanding, one last issue remains: what does the future of the international business environment hold?

Looking into the Future

Perhaps the single biggest challenge in successfully navigating the international business environment is trying to get a handle on the future. If finding a way through the uncertainty of the present weren't enough, the discussion throughout this book has focused on the dynamic nature of the different components of this environment. This means firms must be prepared to look forward and try to accurately gauge what the future might hold, often in a market that is not fully understood. Looking into the future is absolutely essential, but it is not easy; it means being proactive, which is difficult and often associated with high levels of risk. However, failure to do so will inevitably lead to poor performance.

Therefore, before attempting to address the future in terms of the international business environment and its various parts, it is helpful to understand some basic tenets of dealing with the future. First, looking into the future often takes on a projective quality. That is, there is a temptation to extrapolate current trends, which is roughly analogous to driving a car by looking through the rearview mirror. From a logical point of view, there is a reasonable basis for this approach in that it operates under the assumption that the future evolves from circumstances in the present. However, this perspective does not take into account the impact of unanticipated outside "shocks." New applications for new technologies would be one example, but those are, perhaps, easier to anticipate because they tend to be evolutionary in nature. There are, however, outside shocks that are much more difficult to see on the horizon. For example, the often discussed but not yet experienced global viral epidemic spread virtually overnight through air travel (e.g., the anticipated SARS epidemic from years past that never happened). Alternatively, a research breakthrough that could alter the landscape of the international business environment, such as a cure for AIDS and its impact on African economic development, would be profound. Learning from the past is important, but the possibility of the unanticipated is as well.

There is also the problem of being excessively reactive. In the discussion of how to deal with competing firms, it was clear that simply following may be the worst way to deal with the unknown. Assuming someone, or some other firm, can anticipate the future—and also formulate the best course of action—can be dangerous. Analyzing different scenarios is always a better course of action than assuming someone else has a better vision when it comes to knowing the future. Finally, any attempt to anticipate the future will naturally generate debate within any organization. These discussions can create uncertainty, and uncertainty breeds reluctance, which, in turn, impedes decision making. Managing the future is fundamentally fraught with uncertainty, but just as uncertainty related to the international business environment should not prevent a firm from entering into international operations, so too should the uncertainty related to the future not prevent active planning that incorporates change over time. With this in mind, the issue of dealing with the international business environment turns to what are the key areas likely to have a significant impact in the future.

The Regional Perspective

In dividing the global marketplace into geographic regions, one traditional approach has been the East-West perspective. This was a product of the Cold War and predicated on the notion that the more economically developed West (including Japan) dominated the less developed East (most notably Eastern Europe, Russia, and China). This East-West paradigm also tended to assume that the West represented inherently more stable and certain operational environments while the East less so. The 21st century has shown this perspective to be somewhat, but perhaps not completely, flawed. It is true that economic development is clearly not the purview of Western markets; China and India have proven that other nations can play a significant role in the world's economy. However, the sustainability of these large, emerged nations could be questioned. For example, in a few short years, China has gone from being self-sufficient in oil to importing upward of 40 percent of its petroleum needs. Similarly, the recent massive blackouts in India are a sign of a market that may have outgrown its ability to operate effectively over time. The real issue is not whether the West will dominate world economic growth as in times of old but the nature of the interactions between the more established economies of the West, the emerging economies of the East, and the nature of their interrelationships.

Financial Challenges

Few items have dominated the international news of late more than the global financial crisis—in particular, the ongoing problems in the Eurozone. What had been held up as an unprecedented economic success not many years ago—the creation of a unified European market right down to a single currency (at least across a number of markets)—is now in serious jeopardy of collapse. However, although the unique problems associated with the Euro and the Eurozone are an issue of "have" nations becoming increasingly unwilling to support the "have-nots," the underlying economic and financial problems are not unique to European markets. On the contrary, the entire global marketplace is faced with financial challenges that promise to dominate the international business environment for the foreseeable future.

The single overriding financial issue worldwide is one of debt, on both the macro and micro levels. Both developed and developing markets are saddled with extremely high levels of macro, or national, debt. Changing demographics and improved standards of living mean that populations are aging, which, in turn, demands more resources (e.g., health care) be diverted to older individuals. Coupled with the expensive social networks in many of these markets, governments are having, and will continue to have, difficulty meeting obligations to these people. But the problem does not stop there. There is the additional burden of education and infrastructure improvements, national defense, and the financial commitments governments made in years past in an effort to keep economies from spiraling into an even deeper depression. Taking all of this into account, the picture for the immediate future is a sobering one as governments struggle to maintain some semblance of economic growth with few resources to draw on.

There is also the problem of micro debt, especially within the all-important developed markets. In the past, consumers in these developed markets were looked to as a source of economic growth based on their ability to consume more and more product. Unfortunately, the economic crisis of the early part of this century revealed the degree to which relying on these consumers was unsustainable. Although on the surface, there appear still to be high levels of wealth in many of the developed markets, the truth is that high levels of personal debt soak up much of that income. In addition, there is the ongoing problems in the real estate markets—a previously "bullet-proof" form of personal wealth-building that has also eroded. The bottom line is that many consumers in developed markets are at a plateau in terms of increasing individual wealth and the accompanying spending that goes along with wealth growth. Although there are encouraging signs from the perspective of economic growth in many of these markets, it will be a long time before consumer spending reaches the levels of the previous decade.

Social Issues

Several social trends will also serve to increase the uncertainty associated with the international business environment. One of these is the discrepancy in demographic trends, particularly in population trends between developing and developed markets. On the one hand, in developing markets, there are relatively high birth rates, but these are coupled with high levels of childhood mortality, which will demand significant resources if the trend is to be changed. This becomes a catch-22 because devoting resources to health care concerns diverts them away from areas associated directly with economic growth; yet at the same time, a reliable source of human capital is essential for economic growth. Thus, many developing nations will find that moving up the development curve will be increasingly difficult. On the other hand, in developed nations, the problem is just the opposite—but the outcome is similar. These markets show a decrease in birth rate and a steady increase in the age of population. This means less human capital for future growth and the need to apply other resources to support an aging populace. In the end, although different, both trends signal the need to use a substantial amount of already-limited resources in areas other than those directly associated with economic growth.

Another problematic social trend is the polarization of wealth in all markets. This is true between markets—as the European Union has demonstrated. Rather than a relatively even spread across these countries, there are those with high levels of wealth, such as Germany, and those with seriously low levels, such as Greece and Spain. This, in turn, leads to the possibility of increased tensions between markets—a serious problem given the interdependencies that exist in the global market. The problem of polarization of wealth within markets also exists. In both developing and developed markets around the globe, a smaller and smaller group of individuals controls larger and larger amounts of income. The resulting pressure placed on the middle class, generally seen as an engine for economic growth, has been largely negative. Overall, countries can simply no longer depend on the middle class for economic growth, and the polarization of wealth that has caused this problem represents a serious threat for destabilizing even the most developed markets.

A third troubling social trend is both the level, and nature, of unemployment. Unemployment levels are at troublingly high levels—in some population sectors in European countries upward of 50 percent (e.g., people under age 30 in Spain). However, the sheer numbers of unemployed may not be the most worrisome aspect. There are three types of unemployment: frictional, cyclical, and structural. Frictional unemployment is associated with economic activity and is, to some extent, viewed as a positive indicator. Cyclical unemployment, as the label implies, is associated with the ups and downs of the business cycle. Although not ideal, those who are cyclically unemployed stand a good chance of getting their jobs back when the cycle picks up. The most serious is structural unemployment. Individuals who are structurally unemployed generally will not get their jobs back, and, when they do become reemployed, are likely to be underemployed. In many developed markets around the world, structural unemployment is what individuals are facing. The economic destabilization caused by structural unemployment is significant and long term. Although governments talk about job creation, the truth is that even when jobs are "created," many will find themselves at a substantially lower income. Each of these social trends—changes in demographics, unfavorable wealth distribution, and unemployment—all serve to inject high levels of uncertainty into the international business environment and create an even more challenging place for firms to operate.

Technology

A final area to consider is that of technology. The increased efficiencies that go along with technology (productivity, information flow, quality, etc.) are increasingly available to firms and nations of all types. This, in turn, has contributed to an increased rate of change and the resulting increases in costs such as the required financial investment for acquiring the new technology and the switching costs—both direct and indirect—can be a substantial burden. Followed with this is uncertainty as to which change to adapt and when. All of which leads to instability as both firms and nations attempt to stay at the cutting edge—or close to it. There is no question that technology contributes to increased efficiency and effectiveness. However, it also represents change, which contributes to uncertainty and risk.

Summary

Although the primary focus of this book has been the impact the international business environment has on firm operations, and how firms can understand and manage that impact, it is important that firms recognize the impact they have on the markets in which they operate and how best to leverage that impact. The chapter discusses the different ways in which a firm can be a positive influence in a host market, how to get the most out of that positive influence, and the types of host markets most conducive to outside positive influences. The chapter concluded with a discussion of future trends in the international business environment.

A Framework for Assessing the International Business Environment

Introduction

In this book, we have covered a number of facets of the international business environment. Each chapter has been targeted so that you, the reader, could not only become familiar with the key issues contained within each of these facets but also see how they could potentially affect a specific firm and, perhaps more important, deal with any potential problems in an effective and efficient manner. With this in mind, this appendix is designed to provide a framework to take that established knowledge base and bring together all of the assessment information into a single, comprehensive source. This framework provides a one-stop resource for individual firms to assess the international market, or markets, in which they currently operate or are considering as a new area of operations.

The framework moves point-by-point through each component of the international business environment, starting with the firm's approach to international operations and its overall goals and ending with assessing the competitive environment, with stops along the way addressing every other key issue in the international business environment (e.g., culture, physical, economic, political, legal). Applying careful consideration to assessing each of the following areas will provide a clear picture of the environment facing any given individual firm as well as guidance for how best to deal with the attending challenges.

Assessing Firm Objectives and Perspectives

At the outset, assessing the international business environment must first start with an internal firm assessment. This is focused on two key areas: 1) identifying the firm's objectives relative to any current, or planned, international operations and 2) how those international operations relate to domestic, or already established, market activities. Let's begin at the beginning: why your firm is involved in, or considering, international operations (aka "what is your objective?").

- To increase sales: this is the most common objective for international operations but by no means the only justifiable reason. What is it about international markets that might enable the firm to enjoy more sales opportunities than in the domestic market? Does some sort of latent demand for the firm's product exist? Do cultural differences mean higher demand? Or is there a fundamental shift in the product life cycle that means an extended product life? Regardless of the reason(s), if increasing sales is the objective, the firm must be able to identify specifically why the international market represents a significant sales opportunity.
- To acquire resources: an equally reasonable objective would be to leverage international operations to become more efficient through the acquisition of resources. Often operating in different environments can increase competitiveness when the firm can access resources more easily than if it confines itself to strictly domestic operations. Having made that statement, it is vital to be able to specify exactly what resources can be obtained. These generally fall into one of three categories: physical or manufacturing input (i.e., "tangible") resources, intellectual or process (i.e., "intangible") resources, or financial resources. It is not often any single market can provide all three, so if the objective is to increase efficiencies through resource acquisition, there must be a clear idea exactly what resources can be obtained from a market.
- Diversification: more markets can mean less risk. Although the preponderance of discussions related to the international business environment focuses on increased risks and challenges, there is a good argument to be made that international operations can help to reduce overall firm risk. But like the other two primary objectives for international operations, there must be a clear understanding of exactly what risks might be managed when extending the firm's operation scope to international markets. It could be that the goal is to somehow reduce the impact of sales fluctuations (e.g., seasonal, cyclical), which would be best achieved in a market with the appropriate consumption differences. On the other hand, the attractiveness of diversification could be based on differences across the competitive environments of multiple markets—a very different environmental scenario than one in which consumption differences exist. There may also be differences on the value–supply chain from one market to the next (e.g., diversification of suppliers or retailers), which could

also spread potential risks. Pinpointing exactly how the international market(s) differ in a positive way related to overall risk is the only way to achieve this particular objective.

- Minimize competitive risk: it could also be a firm's goal to leverage market differences to reduce competitive exposure. This could mean gaining knowledge related to competing firms, which can be obtained in a more timely fashion in a particular market such as the competition's home market. Other firms find that expanding markets enables them to leverage brand equity that doesn't exist in their home market. It may also be possible to avoid an adverse competitive situation in the firm's home market by moving to another area of operations.

So Step 1 in assessing the international business environment involves being able to specifically identify what your firm intends to achieve and why that particular goal makes sense. The next key piece is to be able to place the international operations into the context of the firm's overall operations. What approach to international business makes the most sense relative to domestic/existing operations?

- A domestic extension strategy: this involves essentially "extending" the firm's current business model to its international markets. The domestic extension approach makes the most sense when there are no significant differences between markets that relate specifically to the firm's product (note: this is not to say market differences don't exist, just that they are not relevant to the firm's product). This approach also has the least amount of impact on a firm's current operations, requires fewer resources, and is the fastest to achieve. Therefore, this becomes a good choice if market differences are irrelevant and/or time or resource availability is a crucial issue.
- Multidomestic strategy: this approach involves developing a unique business model for each international market. Firms that adopt the multidomestic approach generally have identified a limited number of international markets. These markets are particularly attractive because of their differences from existing markets, hence the need for a singular strategic approach. These expenditure of resources—and this is a very resource-heavy approach—is offset by the long-term opportunities presented by the international markets.
- A global strategy: the global strategy requires the firm to develop an approach that is essentially universal, requiring only "fine-tuning" as the firm moves from one market to another. On the surface, this looks much like a domestic extension strategy, but there is a crucial and fundamental difference: it is not built around what works best in the home market but the simple universal similarities that exist across all markets—home and host—in the context of the specific firm and its product offering(s). The firm that can develop a true global strategy can experience a number of advantages, but it is necessary to be able to identify accurately an actionable number of similarities across all markets of operation—not an easy task.

Assessing the International Business Environment—Step 1: Firm Strategy

- What Is Your Firm's International Objective(s) and Why?
- How Will Your Firm Reconcile Its Domestic/Current Operations and International Operations?

Assessing the Cultural and Social Environment

Once the firm has a clear idea as to why it is operating, or considering operating, internationally and what that means for its current operations the next step is to assess the cultural and social context of the host market(s). This involves not only developing an understanding of the composition of that culture and how it will affect external activities such as interacting with customers but also the potential impact of these differences on internal activities (e.g., workforce management) and how best to deal with this challenge.

It is important to remember a few of the basics of culture before assessing its possible impact on an organization. First, culture is not static—it is constantly evolving and does so because of many outside influences including businesses. This means even firms outside of the culture can be influencers. Second, just because cultural differences exist does not mean they are relevant to your firm or its products. A common error is for companies to identify cultural differences in a host market and adjust their approach to that market on the basis of those differences when, in fact, the differences are irrelevant. Third, differences that are relevant are not necessarily threats—they can represent long-term opportunities for product development and enhancement, improved organizational efficiencies, creation of economies of scale, and so on.

With these things in mind, let's look first at how to assess the composition of a host culture. Any culture comprises of five "ingredients," or sets of values: 1) material culture, 2) social culture, 3) the natural world, 4) aesthetics, and 5) language. By simple observation and the use of secondary sources, it is relatively simple to develop a basic understanding of another culture. Remember—this is not about becoming an expert on that culture. Rather, it is about creating a basic foundational understanding.

- Material culture: this is the values, meanings, and emphasis placed on the tangible in a culture. Another way to look at this would be the culture's level of materialism. Relatively high levels of materialism often are associated with a marketplace having cultural differences that may be easier to bridge. Consumers in a materially based culture understand the notion of acquiring new products, and employees in this type of context can be motivated with extrinsic rewards. An emphasis on material culture can be assessed through observations in the market (e.g., the amount of advertising, the message, emphasis on brand names and branding, and the depth of product line choices).

• Social culture: this is the values, meanings, and emphasis placed on the intangible—most notably, human-to-human interactions. These types of cultures can be more difficult to deal with, especially for firms coming from a more materially oriented market (e.g., American businesses). Consumers in these types of markets tend to have a higher level of social awareness in terms of their consumption (e.g., they may purchase a product not because of the brand name but because it enhances social relationships and responsibilities, such as being safer). Employees in a socially oriented culture often place more emphasis on intrinsic rewards than those in material cultures.

• The natural world: while it would be accurate to conclude that this is where religion fits into the discussion of culture, the natural world component of cultural values is more than just religion. Values related to the natural world focus on the relationship between the tangible/real-time experience and the intangible/future experience of human existence. This can affect anything from the role of products in a culture and the types of products that are acceptable, to the types of messages that consumers might accept more readily. These values help "place" individuals in a particular culture into a context where they can understand their role in the world around them; the activities of firms can assist in that contextualization.

• Aesthetics: the term *aesthetics* refers to cultural values related to sensory experiences. This may be the most difficult of the various ingredients of culture to come to terms with because these values are generally not as obvious but are nonetheless powerful influencers. Sights, sounds, and other stimuli provide the basis for how people interact with each other and the larger world itself. In many ways, it is difficult to describe the aesthetic portion of any given culture, but it is a guarantee that violating these values can serve to quickly alienate members of a culture.

• Language: although it may not be considered a "value," language is an important part of culture because it reflects and projects the other cultural values. The language is used to describe the world, human interactions, and virtually everything else; it provides an important insight into how cultures operate. For example, much is revealed about U.S. culture by the language's focus on the individual. Similarly, the precise nature of German culture is reflected in the precise nature of the language itself.

Once there is a basic understanding of the composition of a particular culture, the next order of business is to look at what impact relevant cultural differences might have both on the firm's internal operations—and by extension what can be done to reduce or eliminate any problems—and how these cultural differences might affect the way the firm interacts with the market and consumers in the market. Generally, cultural conflicts within an organization can be traced to one of four basic areas of disagreement.

- Value conflicts/interpretation: as the firm begins to employ, directly and indirectly, individuals from different cultures a variety of cultural conflicts can arise ranging from dealing with customers and suppliers to other employees within the organization. For example, what would clearly be grounds for sexual harassment in the United States or Europe might be viewed as normal interaction in some Asian cultures. These conflicts can quickly turn into ethical dilemmas for employees and must be anticipated to avoid disruption within the firm.
- Concept of structure: although some cultures can be fairly rigid regarding organizational structure, lines of authority, and even the concept of time, it is important to take into account any differences in these areas that might negatively impact morale, decision making, response time, and other issues.
- Concept of rewards: in materially based cultures, motivating and rewarding employees is often built around extrinsic rewards. However, more socially oriented cultures may expect a reward structure that is intrinsically oriented. If there is a cultural disconnect in the reward structure in an organization, managerial decision making can be impeded, and the relevant management tools available may be significantly different from those used in the home market.
- Concept of valuable skills: in Western (i.e., U.S. and European) firms, the most valuable skills are often associated with those directly tied to profit (e.g., sales, finance, accounting). However, other cultures consider those skills directly related to the long-term success of the firm (e.g., human resources) to be the most vital. Different cultures may view employee "value" in different contexts.

The question then arises, how best to deal with these conflict points within an international organization? There are four ways an organization can proactively plan to deal with cultural differences—or more accurately, three ways with ignoring the differences being the fourth.

- A value-based approach: this is when an organization replaces—at least while the employees are at work—individual culture with a corporate culture such as the notion of being an IBMer. This a long-time approach effectively used by IBM over several decades that has successfully survived major overhauls in the organization itself. In effect, a value-based approach builds a strong corporate culture that spans different employee social cultures.
- A process-based approach: organizations with activities that center around a specific process often find they can develop a common technical/professional culture that bridges cultural differences. Within such an organization, the activities of employees cluster around similar processes. For example, Goodyear manufactures more tires than any other company in the world. Its processes can be boiled down to designing, manufacturing, and selling tires. Everyone

within the firm fits into one of these main areas, which means employees in China have more in common with U.S. employees than they might realize and vice versa. Focusing on the process can help reduce cultural conflict points.

- A dependency-based approach: this is where a firm relies on strong financial and/or control systems to manage cultural differences. In essence, this approach requires employees to adopt the existing home-market organizational culture. Although not the most culturally sensitive approach, it is sometimes required when firm growth outstrips the ability to take more time in dealing with internal cultural differences.
- Ignore cultural differences: rarely in business is the recommended course of action to ignore a problem. However, in managing for cultural differences, sometimes—at least at the corporate level—it is advisable not be overmanage. Particularly when it comes to managing individual employees, it may well be that the local managers have the best insight into how to motivate, reward, discipline, or terminate their workers. Perhaps the best means of localizing management styles is to actually leave it to the locals.

The other area in which cultural differences can have an impact on firm operations is in the interaction between the firm and the host consumers in the host market. These activities are focused on the traditional marketing activities: product, promotion, place/distribution, and pricing.

- Product: how might cultural differences affect host consumers' perceptions of the firm's value offering? This could be reflected in different requirements related to the actual product itself (features, etc.), the composition of the product line, product delivery/presentation, and/or product packaging changes.
- Promotion: how might cultural differences affect the firm's ability to communicate its value offering (i.e., product)? Cultural differences may demand the product be positioned differently (e.g., makeup/cosmetics become skin care products), different interactions in the message presentation, different branding, or different visuals on the product packaging.
- Distribution: different cultures also potentially have different expectations regarding distribution strategy. The first issue to address is the perceived role of distribution: is it seen as cost-added or value-added? Western cultures often view distribution as cost-added and seek to "cut out the middleman." However, it may be that choosing the proper distribution channel enhances the overall value perception of the product, enabling higher prices to be charged. Another potential challenge would be the location in which consumers expect to have the product available (e.g., the role of vending machines in Asia). There is also the issue of the expected contact—more socially oriented cultures may expect human interaction in the course of obtaining the product.
- Pricing: cultural differences can affect a firm's pricing in two basic ways. First, it is important that the price be consistent with the product positioning. Telling customers in a host market the product is both "quality" and "affordable" and

then pricing it using home-market guidelines could irreparably damage the product image. Second, it is also important to take into account any potential country-of-origin effect—positive or negative—in pricing a product.

Assessing the International Business Environment—Step 2: The Social/Cultural Environment

- What is the composition of the host-market culture?
- Where are the most likely internal organizational cultural conflict points?
- What approach would work best for your organization in dealing with these internal conflicts?
- How do any cultural differences affect your product as a value offering?
- Do the cultural differences make it more difficult to communicate about your product?
- Are there differences in terms of where consumers in the host market would look for your product and/or interaction with your firm?
- How might cultural differences affect the price a firm charges (i.e., its ability to convert the value offering to revenue)?

Assessing the Physical Environment

The physical environment can affect firm operations both from the perspective of operating internally within a given market as well as externally in terms of market location. Furthermore, although it is easy to consider the physical environment as characteristics such as climate and topography, any assessment of the physical environment also extends to the individuals who live in that market and the infrastructure that exists for implementing business activities. The primary elements to consider in the physical environment are the following:

- Location: what are the neighboring markets? What are the existing trade and political relationships?
- Topography: what are the physical characteristics of the market and how might that affect firm operations (e.g., distribution)?
- Climate and environment: how might the seasonal cycles affect firm operations? Product demand?
- Urban geography: what are the patterns of population distribution? Population density? Do these represent an operational opportunity or threat?
- Human geography: what are the characteristics of the population (e.g., demographics, birth/death rate, education, literacy)?
- Infrastructure: what structures are available for implementation of operations (e.g., movement of product, people, information; production capabilities; product usage capabilities)?

- Natural resources: what, if any, resources are unique to that market? Are they available and accessible to your firm?

If the market appears to demonstrate a favorable physical environment, the next step is to evaluate the market in the context of the firm's international operational objectives. That would include taking into account strategic issues (e.g., the role of international activities in overall operations, other markets the firm may already to active in), marketing issues (e.g., location synergies, target markets, production and demand characteristics), and production issues (e.g., ability to reduce time and distance risk, production costs). The market selection process involves the following areas of assessment:

- Market size and sales potential: this would include income indicators, population trends, and level of industrialization, for example.
- External operational ease and compatibility: an assessment of geographic similarities (both proximity and physical characteristics), cultural/language similarities and differences, and market similarities (e.g., level of economic development, demand).
- Internal operational compatibility: an assessment of company capabilities, or lack of, in the market (e.g., necessary language skills), cost of operations and resource availability (financial, knowledge, expertise), and potential internal bureaucratic obstacles and resistance.
- Risk—an analysis of competitive risk (e.g., numbers, market share, priorities, source, etc.), monetary risk (liquidity, stability, etc.), and political risk (e.g., leadership, stability, external relations).

Once a market, or markets, has been selected, the final assessment involves determining the appropriate market entry strategy.

- Exporting: essentially keeps as much operational control as possible in the firm's home market. Recognize that certain tasks will need to be performed in the host market, either by the firm itself or through a third-party. These tasks include product shipment, local distribution, payment collection, administrative and legal tasks, and after-sale support.
- Partnership: cedes some control to a host-market partner in exchange for local competitive advantage. Can be in the form of a "vertical" partnership (e.g., licensing, franchising) or a "horizontal" partnership (e.g., a strategic alliance).
- Foreign direct investment: extends as much operational activity as possible into the host market. The goal is to become as localized as possible (i.e., take the "international" out of international business). Can be either developed or acquired but also has high levels of risk.

Assessing the International Business Environment—Step 3: The Physical Environment

- What are the physical characteristics of the market?
- What is the result of the market selection analysis?
- What is the most appropriate market entry strategy?

Assessing the Economic Environment

Like the other aspects of the international business environment, assessing the economic environment of a market must be done in the context of overall firm objectives. In considering another market, this means having a clear picture of its operational role. Is the market being assessed as an attractive operational location, a revenue-generating location, or both? In the case of the former, issues such as capital availability, infrastructure, labor costs, labor skills, production inputs, and the like would become crucial; in the case of the latter, it would be demand, ability to pay, competition, and product life cycle stages, for example, that would come to the fore. Having a clear understanding of the strategic and operational role that the market might play should be the guiding force behind the evaluation of a host market and its economy.

- What is the primary source of economic activity and growth (primary, secondary, or tertiary)?
- How stabile are those activities and growth?
- Is this growth sustainable (i.e., what is the economic growth fundamentally based on)?
- What is the rate of growth?
- What is the quantity of demand (e.g., population, per capita income)?
- What is the quality of demand (disposable income, income distribution)?
- Are raw materials and production inputs available and accessible?
- What is the quality of the available component materials?
- What are the characteristics of the available labor force (e.g., cost, education, skills, experience)?
- What is the availability of capital, including possible sources and restrictions?
- What, if any, is the government's role in ownership in the firm's specific industry?
- What is the government's role in resource allocation in the economy?
- What is the government's overall role in the economy (i.e., facilitator or provider)?

After evaluating the basics of the potential host economy, the next step is to assess the possible existence, and nature of, any barriers that might impede operations between this and other markets. That means analyzing any trade barriers.

- Do tariffs exist for products entering this market? What type (e.g., percent of invoice, specific duty)?
- Are there any nontariff/quantitative barriers for moving product in and out of this market (e.g., quotas, voluntary export restraints)?
- Do nontariff/nonquantitative barriers exist in the form of government subsidies, preferred procurement policies, customs and administrative procedures, or other standards?
- If trade barriers do exist, what justifications are given, and how does this affect the firm?
- Does the government actively use trade barriers as a policy tool?

At this point, the assessment process has provided a good picture of the potential host economy and any possible barriers for operating between this and other markets. The final step is to assess the barriers to operating within that economy—that is, the competition.

- What is the primary source of competition (host-market firms, home-market firms, or third-market firms)?
- Are there government subsidies or other support available to host-market firms?
- Are there trade advantages available to third-market firms?
- Are there favorable exchange agreements for third-market firms?
- Are there subsidiary and/or joint venture advantages for either other home-market firms or third-market firms?
- Which firms specifically are considered primary competitors in this market?
- How important to these competitors is this market (e.g., level of investment, level of expenditure)?
- What are these competitors' unique strengths?
- What are these competitors' exploitable weaknesses?
- What are the likely future changes in these competitors' strategy and the impact of those changes?

Assessing the International Business Environment—Step 4: The Economic Environment

- What are the characteristics of the potential host market's economy?
- What, if any, barriers exist to operating between this economy and other markets?
- What is the nature of the competition?

Assessing the Political and Legal Environment

The political and legal environments are related but significantly different from the perspective of international business. The legal environment is concerned with the rules and regulations governing business and business operations, whereas the political environment refers to the process through which those rules and regulations are created. By becoming familiar with, and often involved in, the political process, it is possible to proactively manage the outcome (i.e., the legal environment). To accomplish this effectively, the firm must first understand the nature of the political environment in a host market. This means understanding the role of both government (politicians and civil servants) and nongovernment (opinion leaders and special interest groups) influencers in that market. In some markets, each of these groups may be relevant forces; in others, they may be more or less influential—or perhaps even nonexistent.

This can be most effectively done by putting these groups of potential influencers into their proper context in that host market; that is, establishing how power is exerted within the host market. Political power can be exerted within another market through what would be familiar means to companies coming from developed markets (e.g., constitutional monarchies and constitutional republics), or it may be the case that power is exerted in a less familiar context (e.g., traditional monarchy, a theocracy or quasi-theocracy, or a centrally controlled government). Being able to define the nature of the political environment is the key first step in being able to navigate that environment successfully. Once the underlying nature of the political environment is established, the firm can undertake the task of assessing its potential vulnerability to political risk.

This assessment starts first with an evaluation of internal or firm-specific issues that might make an individual company more vulnerable to political risk. A "yes" answer to any or all of these questions means the firm may be politically vulnerable.

- Is the firm involved in political debates (i.e., does the firm's product or means of doing business potentially create controversy in the political environment)?
- How "essential" is the firm and its product to the host market?
- Do the firm's operations mean involvement—direct or indirect—with the media and mass communications?
- Will the firm's operations have a negative impact on local firms or the local economy?
- Is the firm's primary product a service?
- Is the firm's product potentially hazardous? In what way (e.g., physical hazards, social hazards)?

This internal analysis of the firm in the context of the host market's political environment is just one side of the vulnerability assessment. The firm must also take into account external (market-specific) characteristics of the host market.

- What type of government is present?
- How stable is the government?
- What is the government's level of involvement in the economy?
- What is the market's attitude toward "foreign" firms and their products?
- What is the state of relations between the host- and home-market governments?
- Are there any administrative procedures that would significantly impede operations?

For a firm that determines the possibility for substantial political risk exists in a host market, the question becomes how best to deal with these risks. For the proactive firm, two options are available. The first would be an internal focus in which the firm alters its operations to manage its political vulnerability.

- Seek out some type of joint venture in the host market
- Keep proprietary resources in the home market
- Increase host market levels of dependency on the firm
- Adopt a low profile and/or geographic diversification strategy
- Push future benefits (i.e., be a "good citizen")

Alternatively, a firm might decide to take an external focus. This puts the firm directly into the political process. The goal is either to forestall a political threat or to absorb the source of the threat. A forestalling approach is most effective when the threat is viewed as impermanent (i.e., a shift in the political landscape such as a change in administration could lead to the threat disappearing). An absorption approach is best employed when the threat is seen as more permanent and targeted at bringing the best interests of the firm in line with the best interests of the influencer(s) in the political environment from which the threat originates. As is the case of the internal focus, there are a number of options available to firms seeking to implement an external focus for managing political risk. These include the following:

- Lobbying: establishing direct contact with the relevant elements of the political environment
- Public relations: using indirect influence to manage the political environment
- Political industry alliances: pooling the resources of multiple firms to manage political risks/threats
- Political contributions: either direct (to an individual) or indirect (e.g., Super PACs)
- Government agencies: applying influence and/or as a source of information
- Political inducements: appropriate payments employed in the normal course of doing business within a market

- Establishing "Friendships": direct relationship between the firm and the relevant individual influencer(s) in the host market

Assessing the International Business Environment—Step 5: The Political and Legal Environment

- Who are the relevant influencers in the political environment?
- What is the nature of the political environment (i.e., how is power and authority exerted)?
- Do internal, firm-specific issues exist that would increase the firm's political vulnerability?
- Do external, market-specific, issues exist that would increase the firm's political vulnerability?
- What is the best option for the firm to manage any political risks (i.e., an internal or external focus)?

Assessing the Competitive Environment

The final piece involves assessing the competitive environment. This means not only assessing the so-called traditional competitors but also expanding the firm's thinking and considering other firms that may be involved in the host market that provide competing product offerings. The international business environment is "hypercompetitive," which means not only more market opportunities but more competitors, more risk, more operational uncertainty, and all in a context in which old ways of succeeding are becoming less effective. With this in mind, the successful firm will be one that can quickly identify not only its competitors but also exactly what makes those firms a threat and, by extension, how to gain and hold competitive advantage. The process begins by identifying the competition (i.e., which of the following types of firms are most likely to be encountered).

- New entrants: these are firms that are new to a market and are able to operate more efficiently, provide better products, and/or are motivated to grab market share (i.e., have a lower price).
- Suppliers: not always seen as a "competitor," suppliers can be a negative competitive force when they raise prices or lower quality.
- Buyers: customers are also not generally viewed as a competitive force but can become one when they demand better quality, better service, or lower prices.
- Substitute products: these can be especially challenging in a host market (i.e., a market in which the product is viewed from a different value perspective).

When substitute products require little or no switching costs, are offered at a lower price, are of better quality, or show improved performance, they become a serious competitive threat.

- "Traditional" competitors: competing against firms with a similar product offering can become problematic when a firm has no resource advantage, in a slow growth industry, when high fixed or other (e.g., storage) costs exist, when there is a lack of differentiation, or high exit barriers are present in the industry.

To avoid the problems these competitors represent, the firm must establish competitive advantage in the host market. This competitive advantage is built around understanding the customer, understanding the firm, and then matching customer knowledge with firm capabilities. Understanding the customer involves the following:

- Understand the concept of "value": this means identifying what the firm does well that matters to the customer, how best to apply organizational processes to provide that value, and creating a culture that is both service oriented and innovative.
- Accept that customer perception is reality: host- and home-market customers may seek different values from the same product, and they act on what they think they know, not necessarily objective knowledge.
- Competitive advantage does not stop with customer satisfaction: in a host market where the firm is often on the outside looking in, it is vital to continue beyond having satisfied customers and seek to surprise or delight them.
- Listen to the customer: customer stories are an excellent way to learn how different customers might seek out different values. This can be done proactively (e.g., focus groups), but customers can also tell a "story" when they are observed using the product.

Developing an understanding of the customer, or customers, in a host market is vital but not sufficient. The firm then needs to systematically consider its capabilities and points of differentiation; that is, the firm needs to have a clear understanding of itself.

- Identify core capabilities: at what is the firm especially, perhaps exclusively, proficient?
- Differentiation opportunities: to what extent can the firm's core capabilities be leveraged to create synergistic competitive advantage?
- Establish a competitive identity: using the core and differentiating capabilities, the firm has the option of establishing a competitive identity either through operational excellence, innovation-based product leadership, or customer relationships.

Assessing the International Business Environment—Step 6: The Competitive Environment

- Who is the competition in the host market (i.e., who provides a competing value offering)?
- What specifically do these firms do that makes them a competitive threat?
- What does your firm do particularly well that matters to host-market customers?
- What "values" does your firm provide that the host-market customers will seek out?
- What is the best means of communicating directly with the host-market customers?
- What are the firm's core capabilities?
- How can these core capabilities be leveraged to create differentiation capabilities?
- What is the most effective competitive identity for the firm?

Summary

The successful international firm is one that can come to grips with the many challenges represented by the international business environment. This can be a daunting task. In this appendix, a framework designed to assess systematically the various facets of the international business environment of any given market was outlined. By dealing with each piece of the environment separately, a firm will be in a better position not only to understand but also to manage its international operational activities. The result of the assessment framework provided here is a comprehensive basis for firms of all international experience levels to develop a successful international strategy.

Bibliography

The 10 Lenses: Your Guide to Living & Working in a Multicultural World by Mark A. Williams (Capital Books).

Assessing Financial Vulnerability: An Early Warning System for Emerging Markets by Morris Goldstein, Carmen Reinhart, and Graciela Kaminsky (Institute for International Economics).

A Basic Guide to Exporting by The U.S. Department of Commerce (McGraw-Hill).

Breaking through Culture Shock: What You Need to Succeed in International Business by Elisabeth Marx (Nicholas Brealey Intercultural).

Bridging the Culture Gap: A Practical Guide to International Business Communication by Penny Carte and Chris Fox (Kogan-Page).

Communicating Globally: An Integrated Marketing Approach by Don E. Schultz and Philip J. Kitchen (McGraw-Hill).

Competitive Strategy by Michael Porter (Free Press).

The Cultural Dimension of International Business by Gary P. Ferraro (Prentice-Hall).

Dictionary of International Business Terms by John J. Capella and Stephen Hartman (Barron's Educational Series).

Doing Business in Emerging Markets: Entry and Negotiation Strategies by S. Tamer Cavusgil, Pervez N. Ghauri, and Milind R. Agarwal (SAGE Publications).

Entry Strategies for International Markets by Franklin R. Root (Jossey-Bass).

Essentials of Supply Chain Management by Michael H. Hugos (Wiley & Sons).

Exporting, Importing, and Beyond: How to "Go Global" with Your Small Business by Lawrence W. Tuller (Adams Media Corp.).

Franchising & Licensing: Two Powerful Ways to Grow Your Business in Any Economy by Andrew J. Sherman (American Marketing Association).

Fundamentals of International Business Transactions: Documents by Ronald A. Brand (Kluwer Law International).

Global Brand Strategy: Unlocking Brand Potential across Countries, Cultures, and Markets by Sicco Van Gelder (Kogan-Page).

The Global Market: Developing a Strategy to Manage across Borders by John A. Quelch and Rohit Deshpande (Jossey-Bass).

Global Purchasing and Supply Management: Fulfill the Vision by Victor H. Pooler, David J. Pooler, and Samuel D. Farney (Kluwer Academic Publishing).

Global Trade and Conflicting National Interests by Ralph E. Gomory and William J. Baumol (MIT Press).

Global Trade Financing by Harry M. Venedikian and Gerald A. Warfield (Wiley & Sons).

Import/Export: How to Get Started in International Trade by Carl A. Nelson (McGraw-Hill).

International Accounting: A Global Perspective by M. Zafar Iqbal (South-Western College Publications).

International Business in the 21st Century by Bruce D. Keillor, General Editor (Praeger).

International Business Negotiations by Pervez N. Ghauri and Jean-Claude Usunier (Elsevier Science).

International Business Transaction: In a Nutshell, by Ralph H. Folsom, Michael W. Gordon, and John A. Spanogle (West Group Publishing).

International Sales and the Middleman: Managing Your Agents and Distributors by John P. Griffin (Management Books).

Inside the World Bank Group: The Practical Guide for International Business Executives by William A. Delphos (World Bank Publications).

The Law and International Business Transactions by Larry DiMatteo (South-Western College Publications).

Practical Guide to U.S. Taxation of International Transactions by Michael S. Schadewald and Robert J. Misey (Kluwer Business Publications).

The Quest for Global Dominance: Transforming Global Presence into Global Competitive Advantage by Anil K. Gupta, Vijay Govindarajan, and Haiyan Wang (John Wiley & Sons).

A Short Course in International Marketing: Approaching and Penetrating the Global Marketplace by Jeffrey E. Curry (World Trade Press).

Strategic Partnerships: An Entrepreneur's Guide to Joint Ventures and Alliances by Robert Wallace (Deerborn Trade).

Using the Web to Compete in a Global Marketplace by Browning Rockwell (John Wiley & Sons).

Winning in the Global Market: A Practical Guide to International Business Success by Bruce D. Keillor (Praeger).

Working Globesmart: 12 People Skills for Doing Business Across Borders by Ernest Gundling (Davies-Black Publications).

Index

About the Author

Dr. Bruce D. Keillor received his Bachelor of Arts (Economics/Japanese Studies) from the University of Minnesota in 1987, his MBA (Marketing Concentration) from Minnesota State University in 1989, and his PhD (Marketing) from the University of Memphis in 1994. In addition to serving as Professor of Marketing and International Business at Youngstown State University (YSU), he is Director of the Williamson Center for International Business. Before joining the Marketing Department at YSU in August 2008, he was, for nine years, Professor of Marketing and International Business, and both Associate Director and Director of the Institute for Global Business at the University of Akron. Over the past 25 years, Dr. Keillor has lived, studied, and worked abroad in Europe and Asia. He served as General Editor for the four-volume set *Marketing in the 21st Century* (Praeger 2007), the three-volume set *International Business in the 21st Century* (Praeger 2011), and is the author of the book *Winning in the Global Market: A Practical Guide to International Business Success* (Praeger 2011). In addition, Dr. Keillor has published more than 100 referred journal articles, conference papers, and book chapters in the past 17 years. His primary areas of expertise are international marketing strategy, global product and brand strategies, cross-cultural research methodology, and global consumer behavior. In addition, he has served, or is currently serving, on a number of review boards, including *Journal of International Business Studies*. Dr. Keillor is also the Founding Editor of the *Journal of Interactive Marketing* (formerly known as *Direct Marketing: An International Journal*) published by Emerald Publications and is a Research Fellow in the Center for International Business at Michigan State University. Outside of his academic activities, Dr. Keillor is an active consultant, with clients that include Fortune 500 firms.

DATE DUE
